MUSEUM DESIGN PROPOSALS

DESIGN MEDIA PUBLISHING LIMITED

©2012 by Design Media Publishing Limited
This edition published in September 2013

Design Media Publishing Limited
20/F Manulife Tower
169 Electric Rd, North Point
Hong Kong
Tel: 00852-28672587
Fax: 00852-25050411
E-mail: suisusie@gmail.com
www.designmediahk.com

Editing: Helen LIU
Proofreading: Katy LEE
Design/Layout: Ning LI

ISBN 978-988-15069-9-3

Printed in China

MUSEUM DESIGN
PROPOSALS

Contents

Musee de Louvain-la-Neuve

Location: Louvain-la-Neuve, Belguim **Designer:** Perkins+Will **Competition Date:** 2009

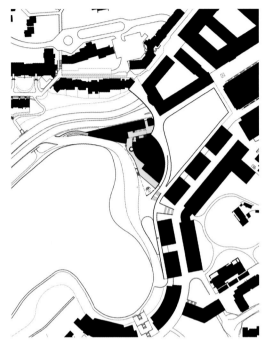

Town entry from west

View from southwest

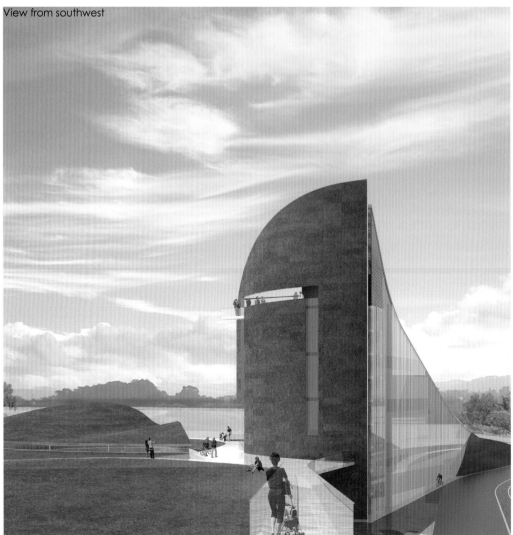

The design of this art museum was driven by the concept of creating a building that would both preserve and extend a new park-like setting along an existing lake while simultaneously acting as an entrance element in the context of the campus master plan. The building acts as a binding element between the urban town centre and a naturalistic lakeside park.

The building consists of two major elements. The first element is an exhibition tower, which houses the museum's permanent art collection, offices and workshops. The second element is a park-covered base containing public functions such as a theme bar, auditorium and temporary exhibition space. The sloping green roof of the exhibition tower grows out of the landscape along the lake and forms an edge along the main town entrance boulevard while creating a more intimate and natural setting about the lakeside.

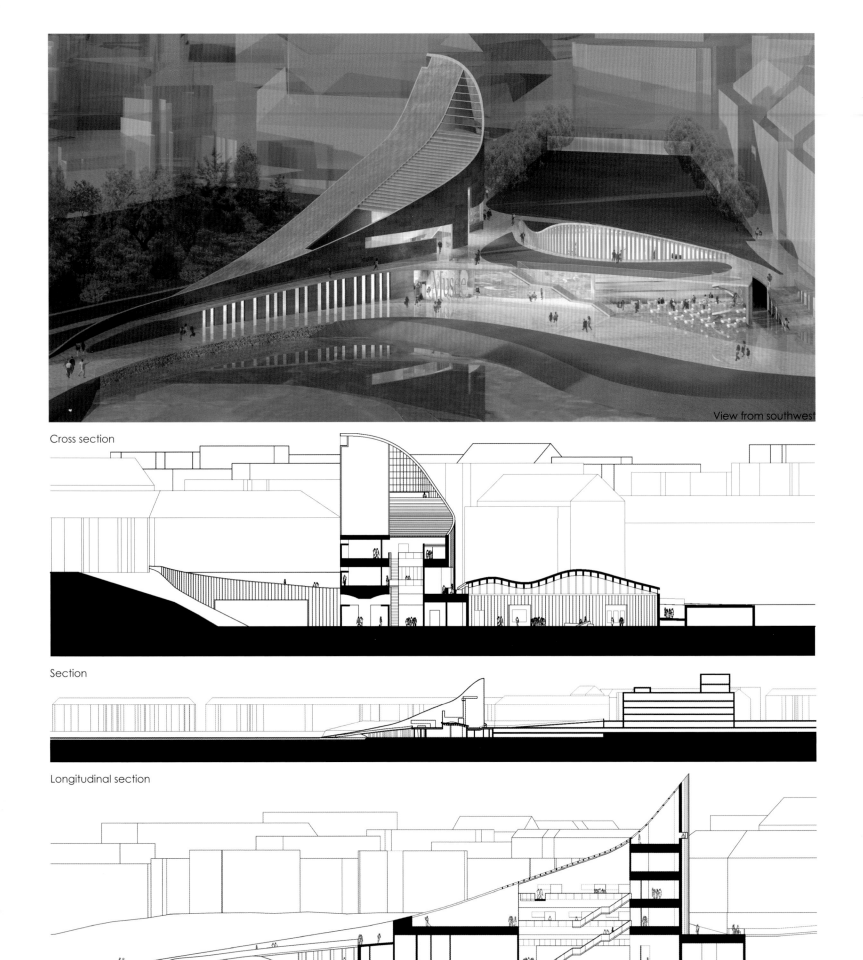

View from southwest

Cross section

Section

Longitudinal section

8

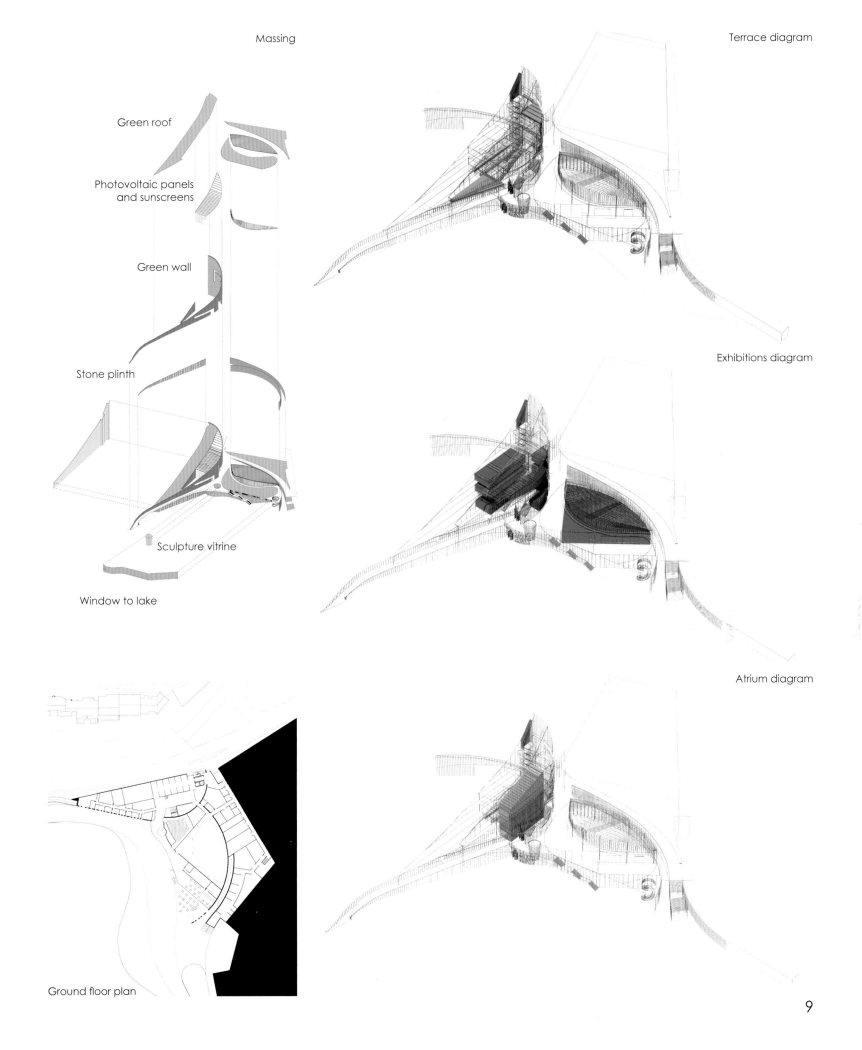

Massing

Green roof

Photovoltaic panels
and sunscreens

Green wall

Stone plinth

Sculpture vitrine

Window to lake

Ground floor plan

Terrace diagram

Exhibitions diagram

Atrium diagram

9

View from southwest

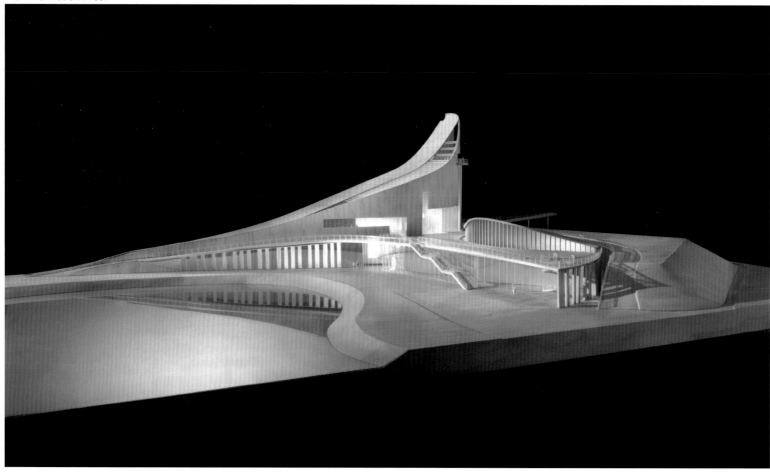

View from west

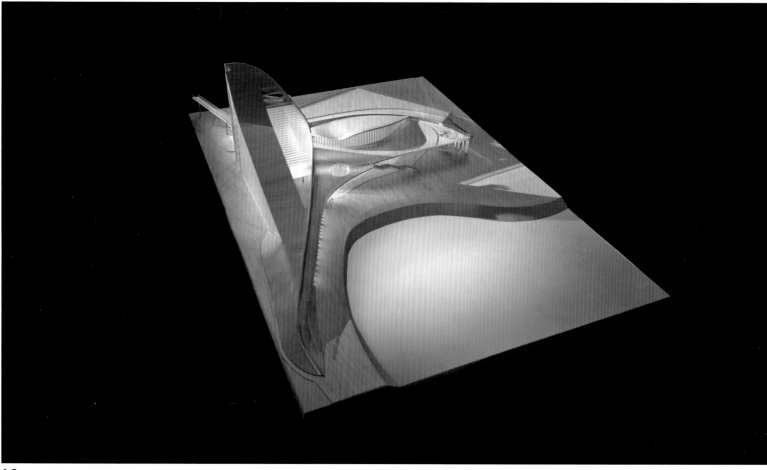

Central exhibition space

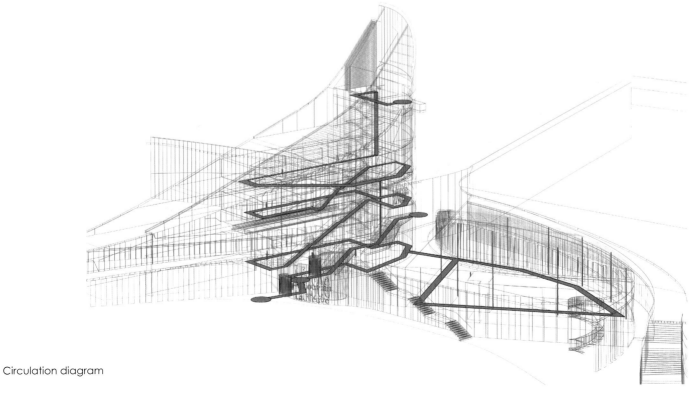

Circulation diagram

Temporary exhibition gallery

Lobby

Central exhibition space

Exhibition gallery

National Art Museum

Location: Nanjing, China **Designer:** KSP JÜRGEN ENGEL ARCHITEKTEN **Photographer:** KSP JÜRGEN ENGEL ARCHITEKTEN **Competition Date:** 2010 **Site Area:** 10, 600 sqm **Construction Area:** 27, 449 sqm **Place in the Competition:** 1st Prize

Awarded reason:
The new Art Museum building responds to the highly historical setting.

The new Art Museum in Nanjing, China lies to the south of the cultural axis that is Changjiang Road and north of the "revolution road" that is Zhongshan East Road.
In planning terms the Museum is a response to the surroundings that are steeped in history: An edifice in the south – the Revolution Cube – adopts the direction of Zhongshan East Road, while that in the north, the Culture Cube, follows the course of Changjiang Road. The space in between the two U-shaped interlaced structures at angles to each other takes the form of a canyon-like access area. The main entrance is located in the northwest and makes a point facing City Plaza. A second entrance in the south delineates the other end of the canyon.

View of square

Overview

14

South elevation

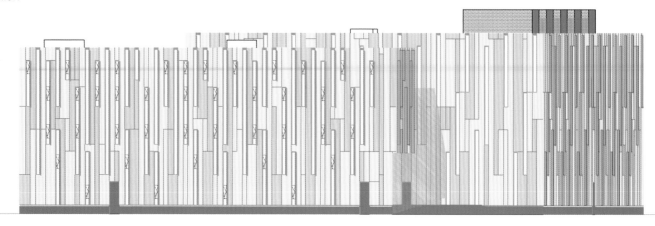

North elevation

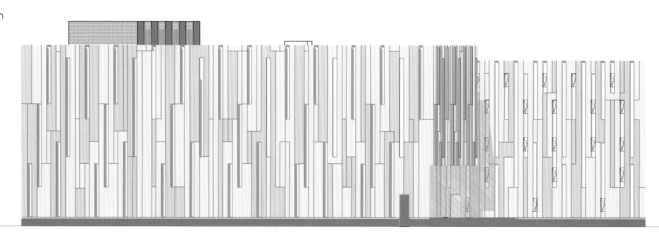

East elevation

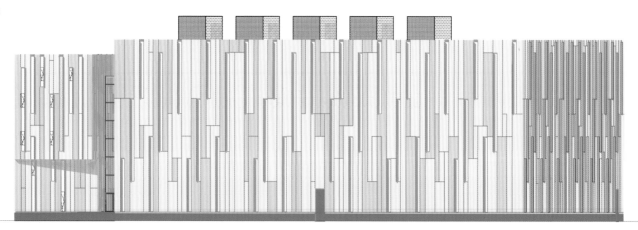

West elevation

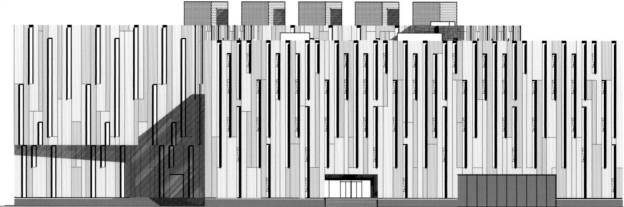

16

17

Outside view

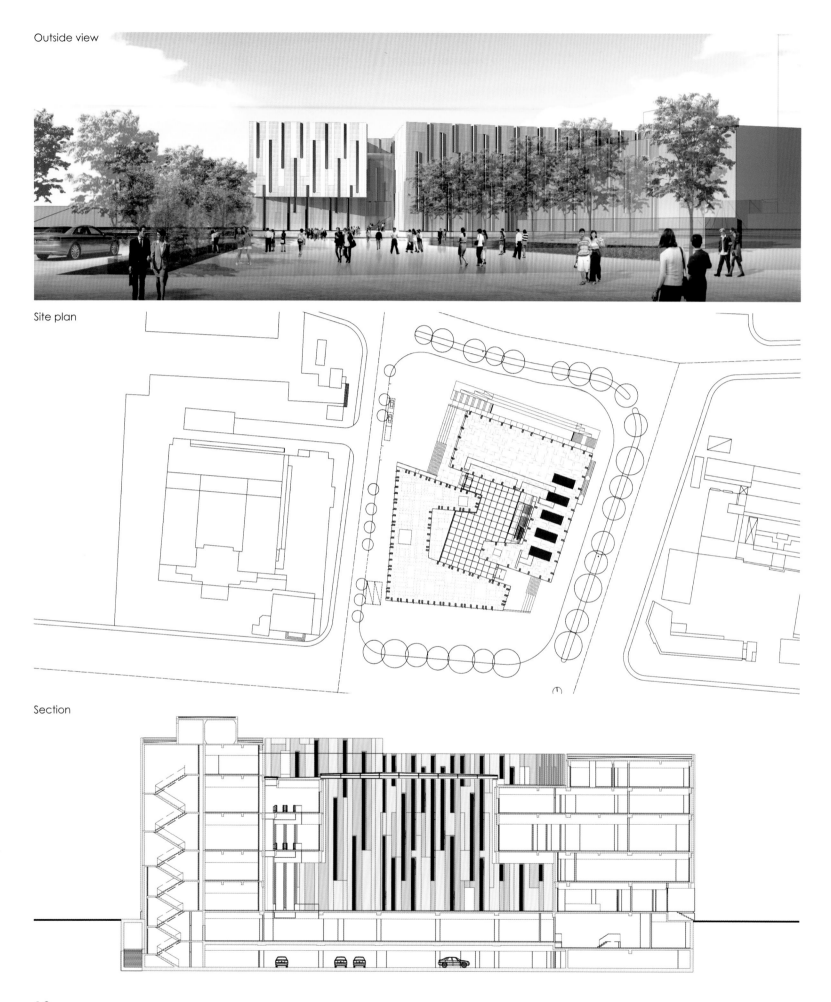

Site plan

Section

Aerial view

Entrance view

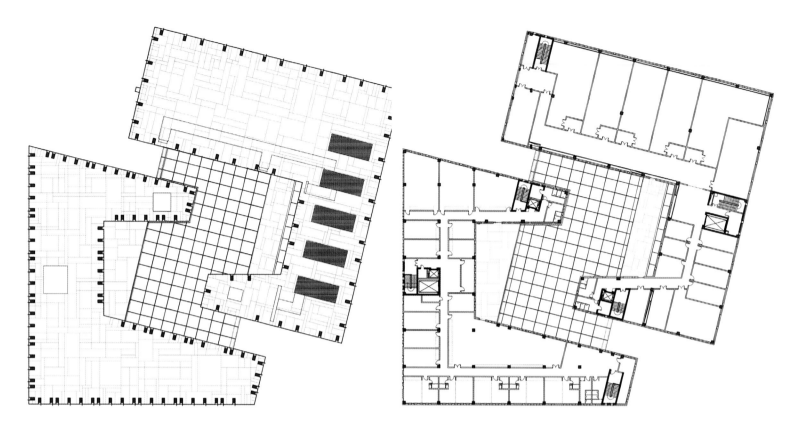

Roof floor plan

Third floor plan

Second floor plan

First floor plan

20

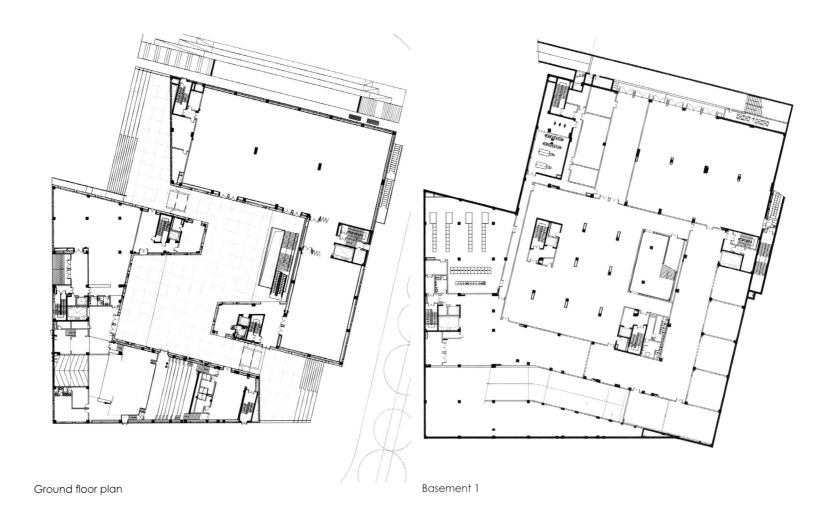

Ground floor plan

Basement 1

Basement 2

Mezzanine floor plan

22

Exhibition hall

Atrium

Yin Yang

Location: Oslo, Norway **Designer:** REX **Competition Date:** 2009 **Competition Name:** Munch Museum and Stenersen Museum Collections **Construction Area:** 16,585 sqm **Place in the Competition:** One of three finalists

Awarded reason:
Their "yin yang" concept offers complete flexibility without increasing operational costs by providing built-in tools.

The "Yin Yang" proposal for the new Munch Museum is strategic, establishing itself as a worthy counterpart by radically addressing two cardinal challenges facing contemporary museum design.

Contemporary museum flexibility is typically conceived as generic white boxes – a blank slate – in which any exhibition format can be constructed. In practice however, as artistic media grow more diverse and museum operational budgets become more limited, a blank slate becomes constrictive: museums cannot afford to endlessly transform their generic galleries. The result is not freedom, but imprisonment within a white box.

By embracing a new form of gallery flexibility, the Yin Yang proposal for the new Munch Museum avoids this trap. Yin Yang offers complete flexibility – without increasing operational costs – by providing built-in tools.

Night time rendering

View from Opera Roof

Combined large gallery rendering

Overall model shot

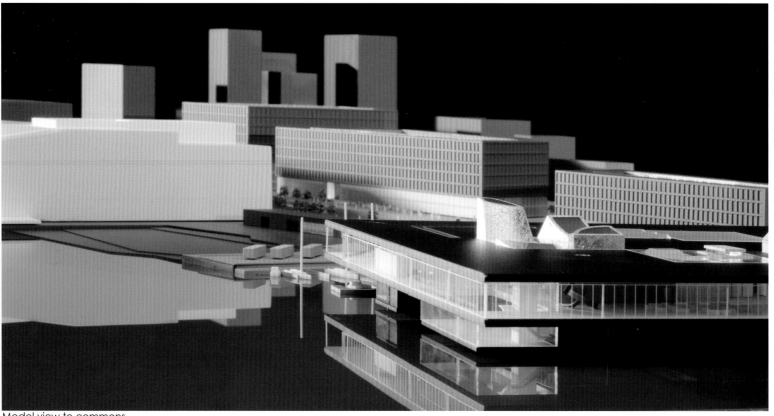

Model view to commons

26

Villa gallery

Universal gallery

Rotating gallery

28

Ground floor plan

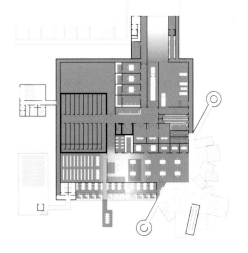

Master plan

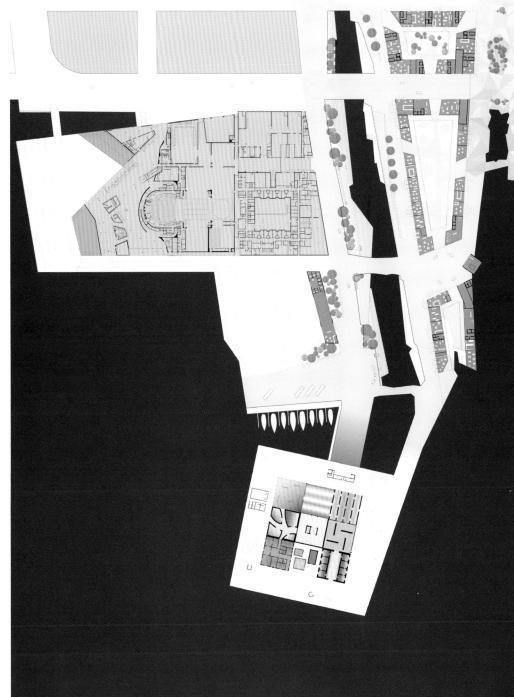

First floor plan

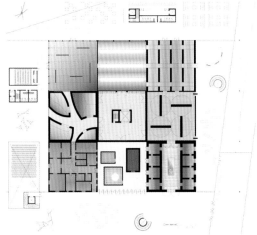

Urban Argument

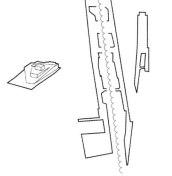

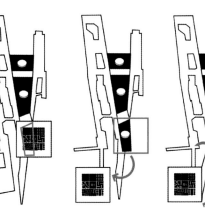

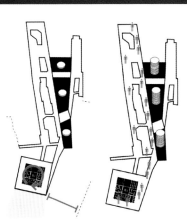
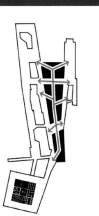
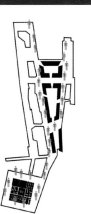
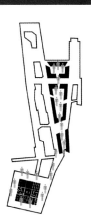

29

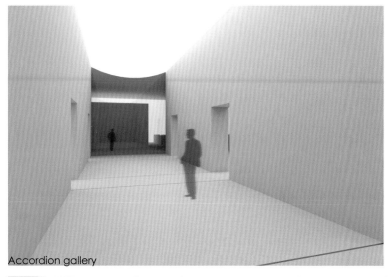

Accordion gallery

Classical gallery

Studios gallery

White Box gallery

Shaped gallery

30

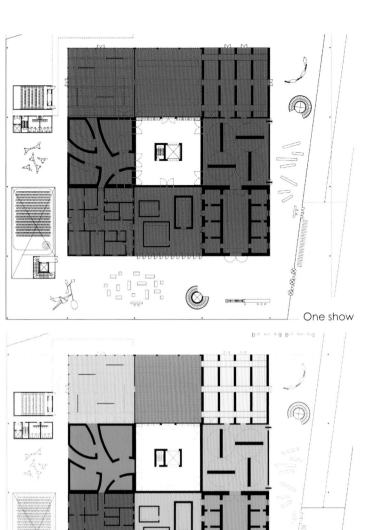

One show

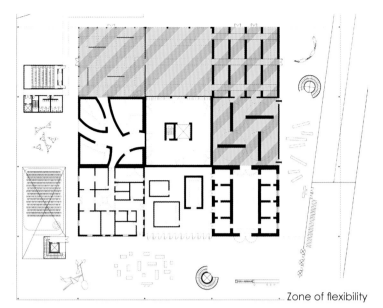

Zone of flexibility

Eight independent shows

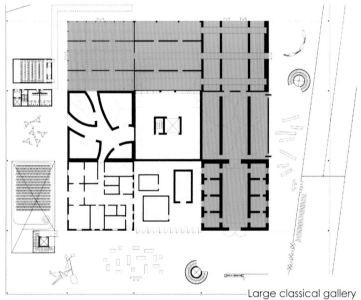

Large classical gallery

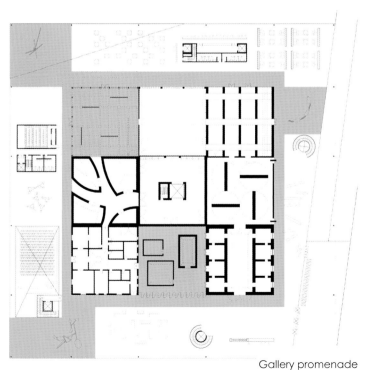

Gallery promenade

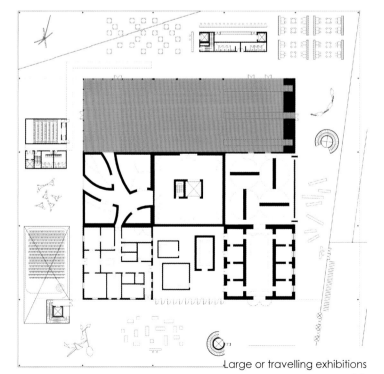

Large or travelling exhibitions

31

Seoul Museum of Art

Location: Seoul, South Korea **Designer:** Yooshin Architects & Engineers **Competition Date:** 2009 **Construction Area:** 13,000 sqm

The proposed Seoul Museum of Art aims to supplement the limited exhibition and storage space existing in Seoul. Apart from providing much needed additional exhibition and art space, the proposed building aims to redress the balance of cultural institutions in the city. The new museum will be located in the North-East of Seoul which is currently lacking any major cultural buildings.

By stratifying the museum into transparent fingers interspersed with courtyards, the building breaks down the clear boundaries between inside and outside. Art located within the courtyards appears as part of the park and the building. Art within the transparent fingers can be experienced from within and from the public park.

By virtue of its massing and its open relationship with the ground, the project becomes porous and permeable, the antipode to the closed black box museums of the past. This architectural porosity will allow residents, curators and artists to find new relationships to artworks, from formal exhibitions to incidental encounters, luring the community inside while letting art escape its traditional confines.

Perspective

The new paradigm of gallery space

Interactive art gallery

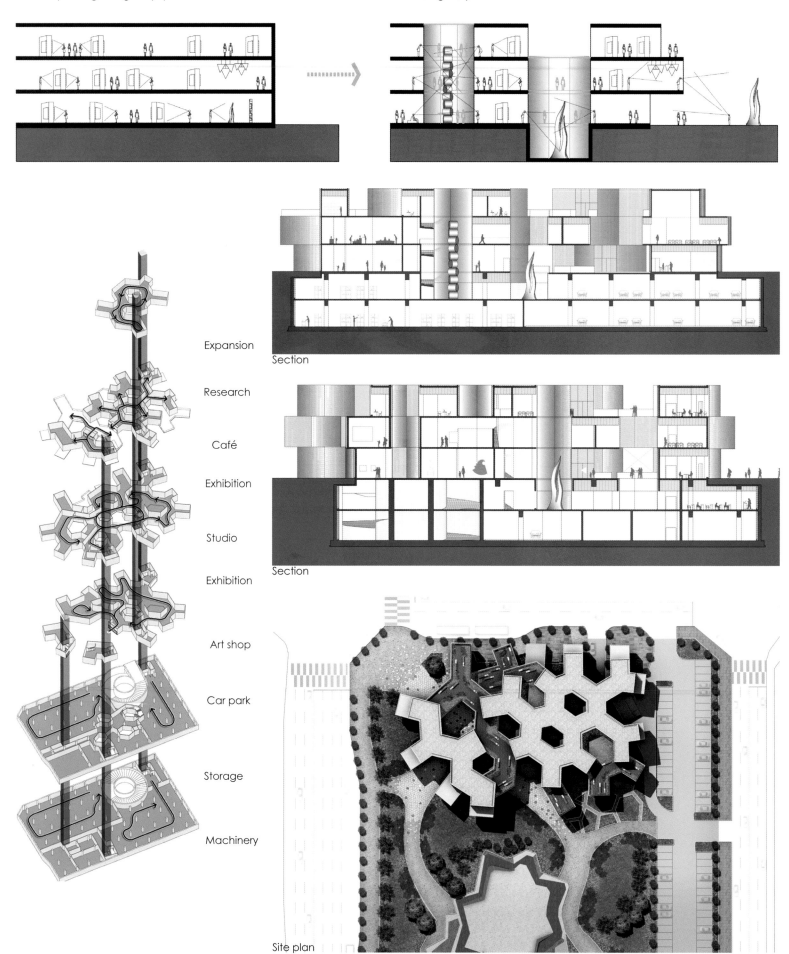

Expansion

Research

Café

Exhibition

Studio

Exhibition

Art shop

Car park

Storage

Machinery

Section

Section

Site plan

Courtyard

35

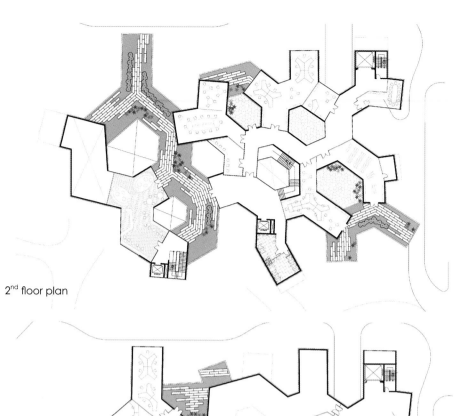

2nd floor plan

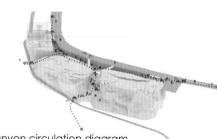

Canyon circulation diagram

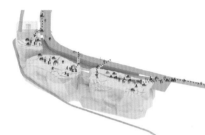

Terrace circulation diagram

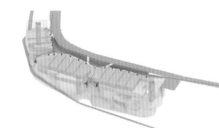

Retail access

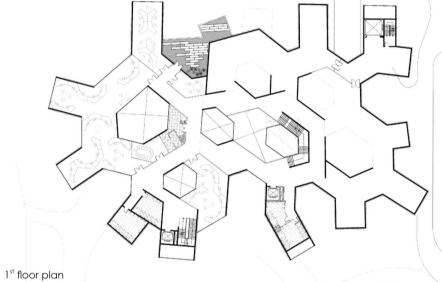

1st floor plan

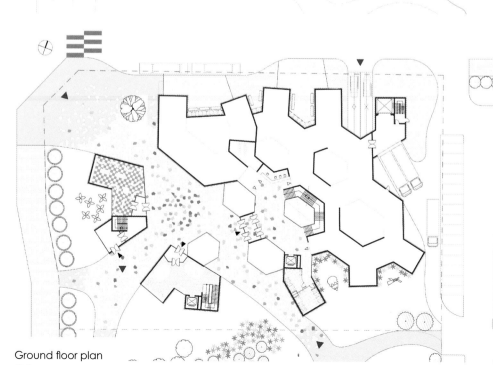

Ground floor plan

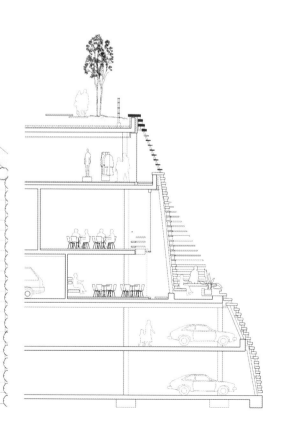

Architectural interpretation of the existing flows

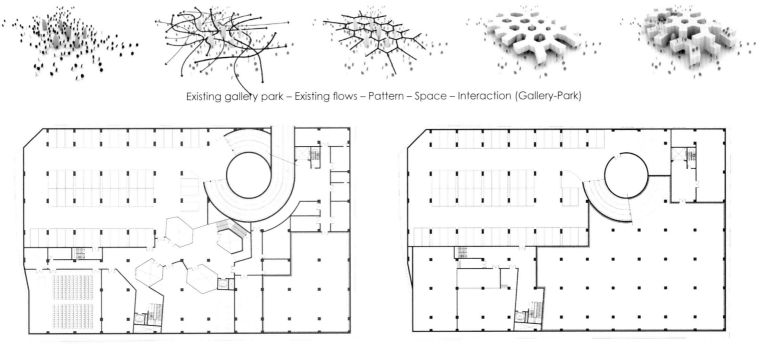

Existing gallery park – Existing flows – Pattern – Space – Interaction (Gallery-Park)

Basement 1

Basement 2

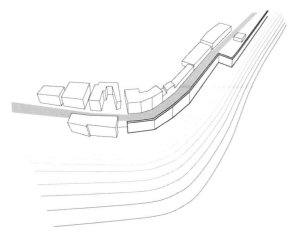

Existing open site condition after carpark demolition

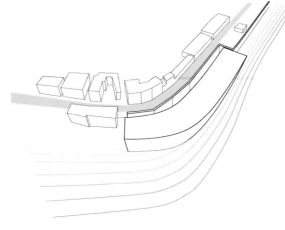

Building massing filling entire site below street level

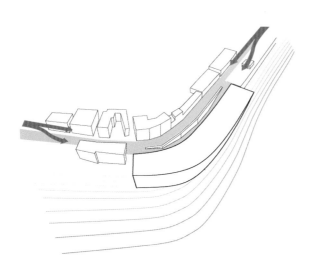

Ramped passage between old city wall and new building

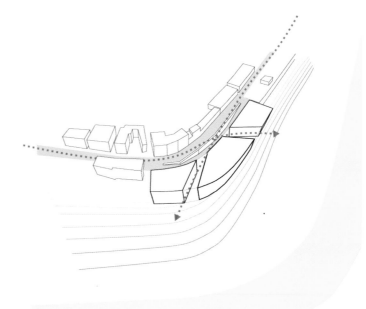

Cuts for view down onto river

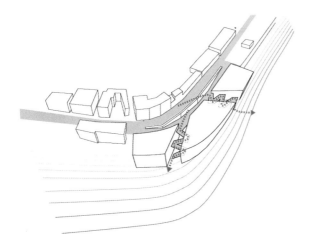

Cuts used for site circulation and function access

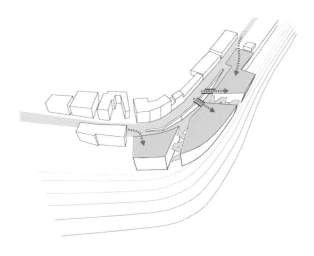

Roof converted to city park terraces

South-eastern entrance to city terrace

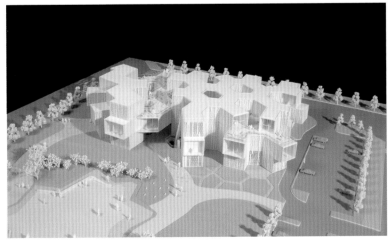

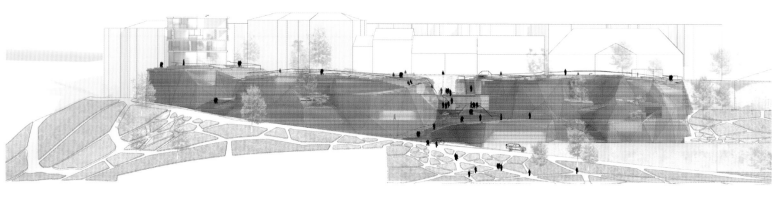

South elevation

North elevation

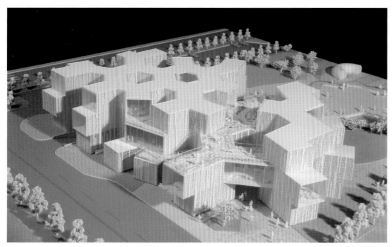

Section

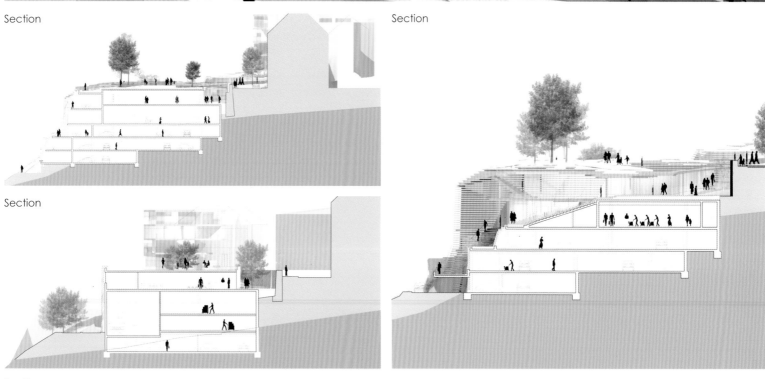

Section

Section

Section

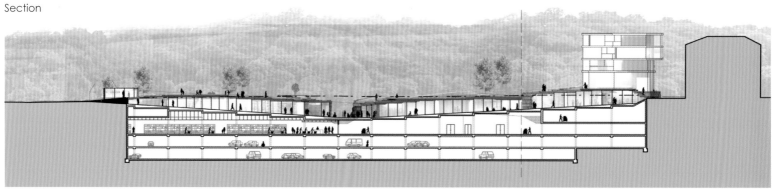

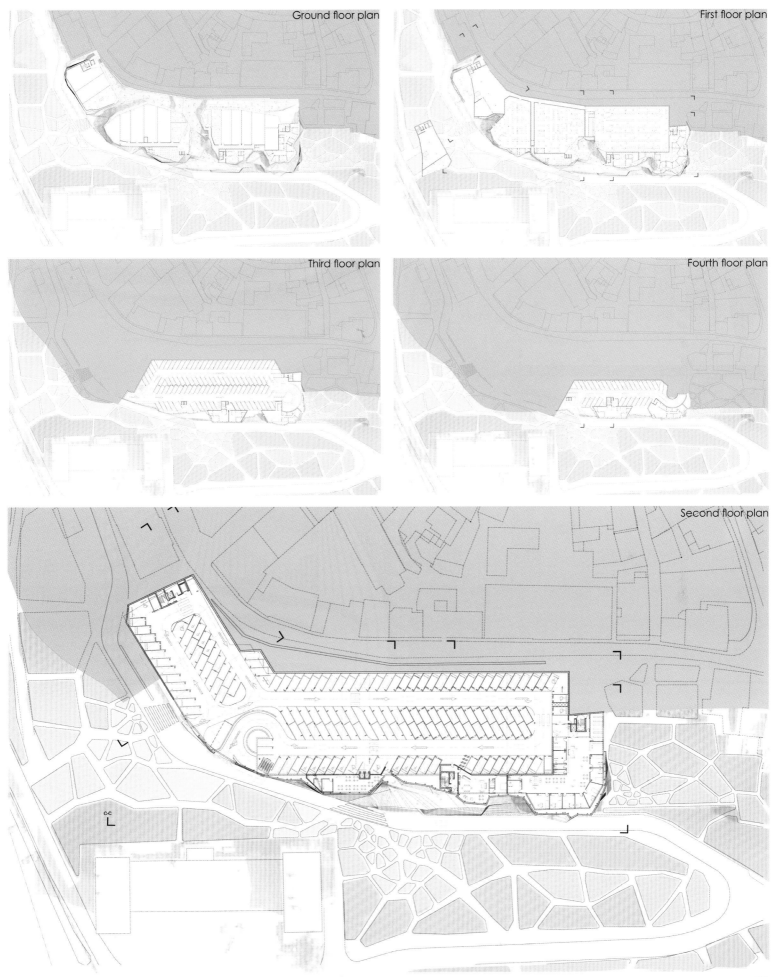

Ground floor plan

First floor plan

Third floor plan

Fourth floor plan

Second floor plan

Breathing Cloth Tower

Location: Tokyo, Japan **Designer:** UNOAUNO - spazio architettura, Marino la Torre, Alberto Ulisse **Competition Date:** 2009 **Site Area:** 403.376 sqm **Place in the Competition:** Honourable Mention

building's terraces with Tokyo skyline in background

Museum exhibition room

View of the outside projecting runway

The building's enervated skin is designed like a breathing cloth, using flaps, folds, and holes; allowing the combination of the inner and outer space, through an osmotic process, where fashion blows in and out through the exhibition rooms. At the same time, this permeable skin allows a complete 360 degree view of Tokyo's landscape at each level of the tower. This breathing skin may also be developed and cut like a paper pattern, just like the clothes. It is perforated by windows with several sizes that give the appearance a fabric feel.

Several cantilevered terraces and the world highest runway (80 metres high) are easily visible from the Omotesando Street (which has become a real fashion street). These terraces seem to get out through swellings of the building skin, as if they came out from the inside of the body.

The vertical museum is organised around a central system of tapis roulant that rises to the full height of the building. Conceived as a stacked vertical piazza, this inner space is designed to promote socialisation and experience sharing among visitors.

The terraces get out through swellings of the building skin

The 1970s style exhibition room and the fashion collection "formindossa"

Tower design is conceived as a dress; in four steps the pure architectural volume was cut and shaped as tailors do with a dress.

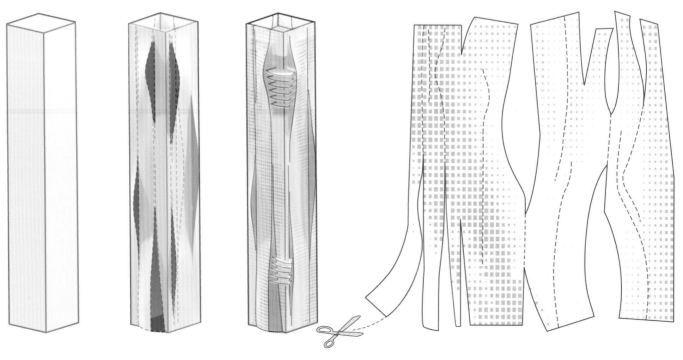

Concept

The view from Omotesando Street

Runway plan

Museum plan

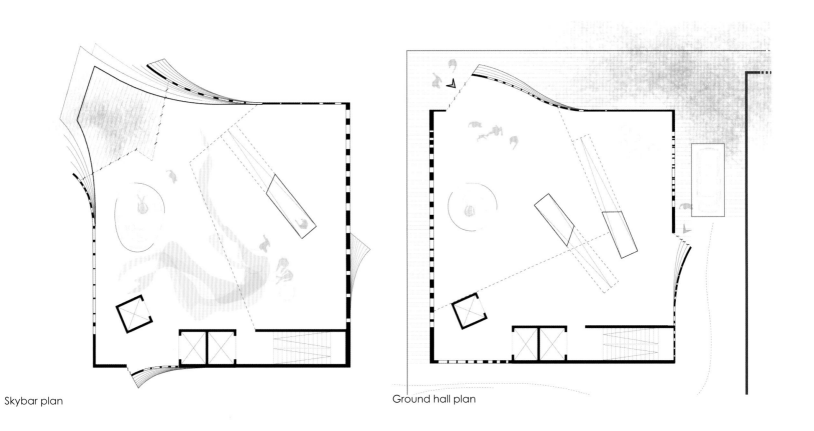

Skybar plan

Ground hall plan

48

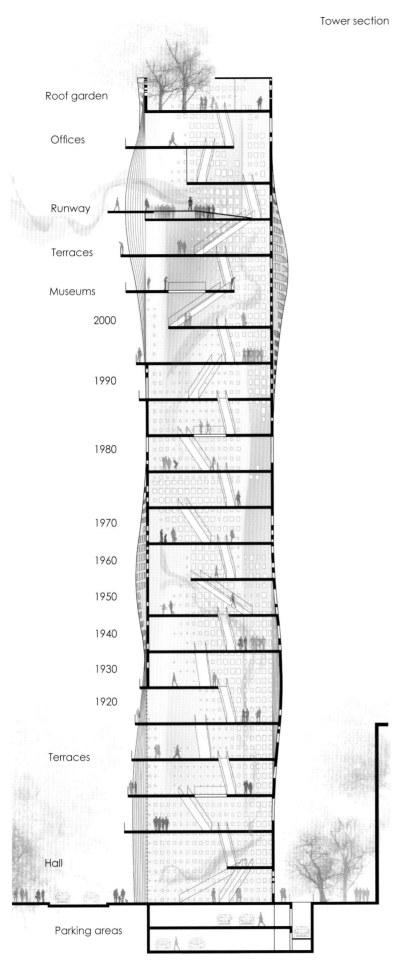

Roof garden

Offices

Runway

Terraces

Museums

2000

1990

1980

1970

1960

1950

1940

1930

1920

Terraces

Hall

Parking areas

Night view of the tower

New Tamayo Museum

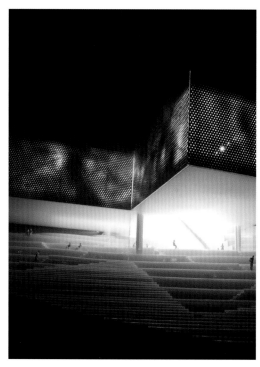

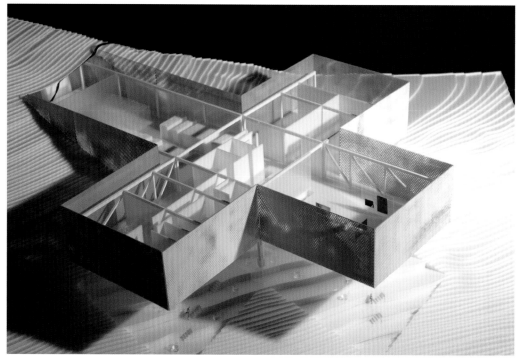

Location: Atizapan, Mexico **Designer:** Michel Rojkind, BIG **Photographer:** Michel Rojkind, BIG **Competition Date:** 2009 **Competition Name:** Museo Tamayo Extension Atizapan **Construction Area:** 3,500 sqm **Place in the Competition:** 1st Prize

Set upon a steep hillside in Atizapan on the outskirts of Mexico's largest metropolis, the New Tamayo Museum will serve as a nucleus of education and culture, locally, regionally, and internationally. Named after the Oaxacan born artist Rufino Tamayo (1899-1991), the very strong and symbolic shape of the cross is a direct interpretation of the client's preliminary programme studies that defined the museum's optimal functionality.

The main concept of Museo Tamayo Extension Atizapan is an "opened box" that unfolds, opens and invites visitors inside. Package, restoration and storage will serve as additional cultural spaces for visitors to understand the stages that an art piece goes through in order to get to its specific destination.

This is a very direct, strong and symbolic project. The shape derives from the client's preliminary studies that defined the optimal functionality and was then enhanced by taking advantage of the best views from above, making the best of the steep terrain and shading the more social programme below. Exterior and interior spaces overlap to provide the best environment possible for each function, and optimal climatic performance.

Night view

Perspective

Access floor plan

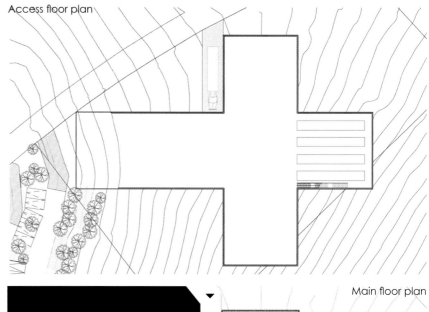

Main floor plan

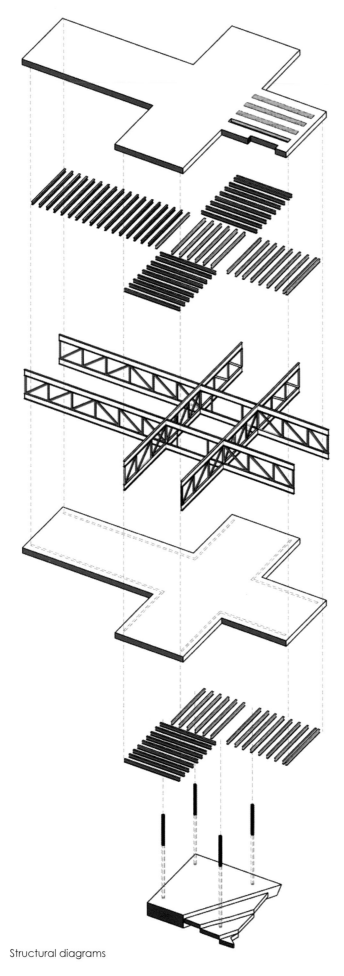

Structural diagrams

52

Roof

Exhibition space

National Museum of Fine Arts of Quebec

Location: Quebec, Canada **Designer:** Saucier + Perrotte architects/Bélanger Beauchemin Morency architects **Photographer:** Saucier+ Perrotte architectes **Competition Date:** 2009 **Competition Name:** International Architecture Competition of MNBAQ **Place in the Competition:** Semi-Finalist

Awarded reason:
The museum project's marked visual and programmatic porosity highlights the important role that this institution plays in Québec's cultural and social landscape, both at local and international levels.

The museum expansion project, a glowing glass object, is grounded into its site, at once anchored to the urban axis of the Grande Allée, while dematerialising to respectfully leave place for the existing museum buildings. The bright and reflective project gives life to its site, both at the day's end and during the grey periods that characterise the colder seasons of Quebec's winter. By varying in its degrees of transparency, the museum allows for different lighting conditions depending on the artwork exhibited, and simultaneously defines various parcours through the site to give visitors a deeper understanding of the landscape and history in which they are immersed.

The project's setback from the Grande Allée is meant to underscore the public nature of the new building. A new public square, framed by the projecting cantilever, emerges off the street to offer visitors an exterior urban space to inhabit before entering the Grand Hall at the heart of the building.

The artwork in the museum occupies spaces characterised by simplicity of formal expression, ample and rectilinear in nature. The structural parti allows for column-free space to permit a large degree of flexibility. The galleries are for the most part made up to opaque partitions, but at the north and south ends of the building, these walls are composed of movable panels, louvres which open the spaces up to the city and river for special exhibitions and events.

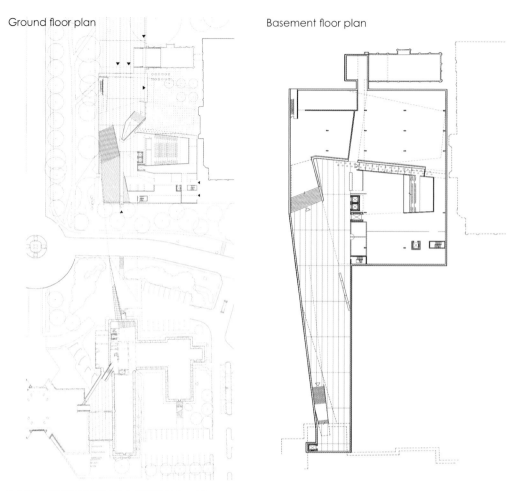

Ground floor plan

Basement floor plan

Grande Allée view

General view

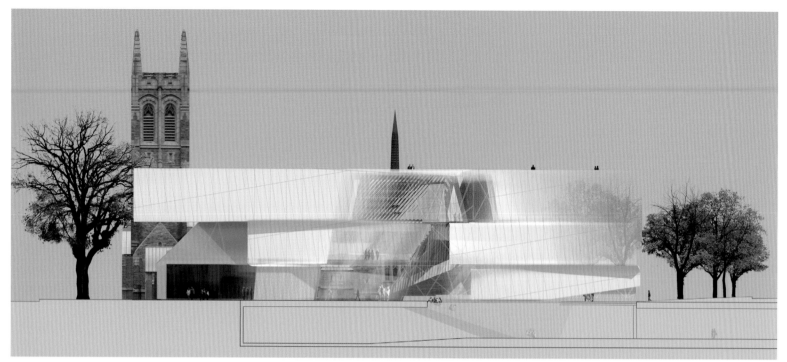

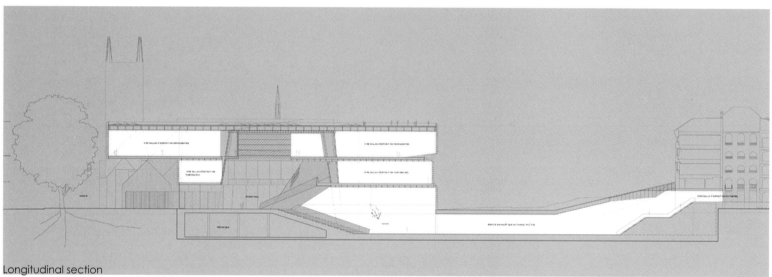

Longitudinal section

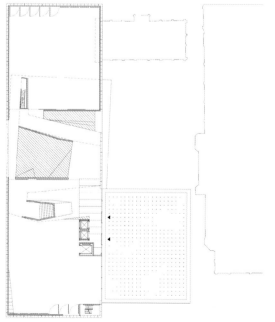

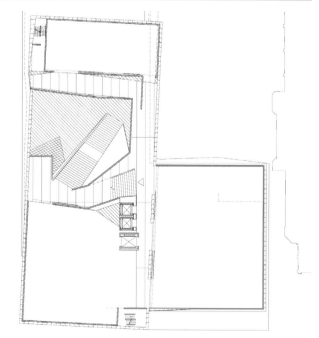

Second floor plan

First floor plan

56

The hall view

The tunnel

Church Street

The gallery

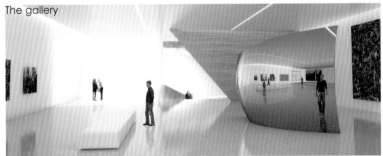

The mezzanine view

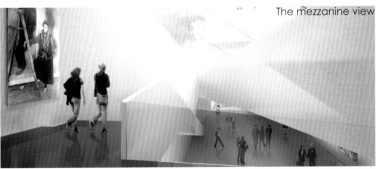

National Museum for Art, Design and Architecture

Location: Oslo, Norway **Designer:** LOOS ARCHITECTS & bureau SLA **Photographer:** Eyal Shmuel/Vingt Six **Competition Date:** 2009 **Competition Name:** International Competition for National Museum for Art, Design and Architecture, Oslo, Norway **Construction Area:** 79,000 sqm **Place in the Competition:** Entry

Awarded reason:
The task of the new museum complex should be to connect in a clever and sophisticated manner to the urban tissue, while at the same time reacting sensitively to the existing buildings on the site.

Situated close to the waterfront the location for the new National Museum of Norway competition occupies a prime position. As a national museum, of course it has to be an icon but not an alien. This competition design fulfills the requirement: It's a new landmark, which not only fits into the city structure, but also complements it. The sculpturally sloping roofline is the characteristic feature of the museum.

It is at the same time a very systematic and a very playful museum design. Based on a triangle motif, it has a very clear identity, without becoming a simplistic logo. Although unobtrusive in silhouette in order to contribute to and blend into the city fabric, its elegantly shiny material and triangular structure make it a recognisable building. This recognisability informs the outside as well as the inside of the museum, making its interior a white cube with identity – tributary to the artworks, but never exchangeable.

Terrace

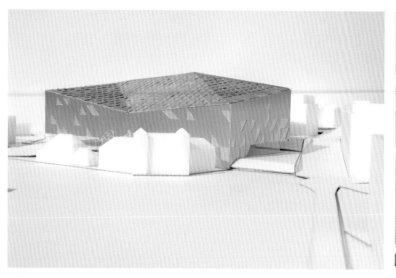
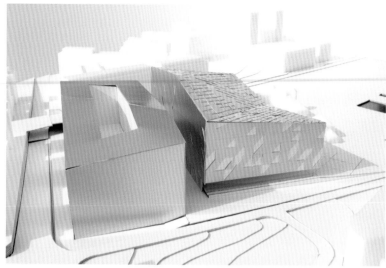

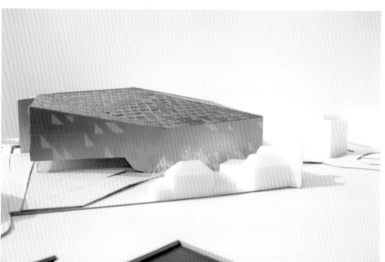

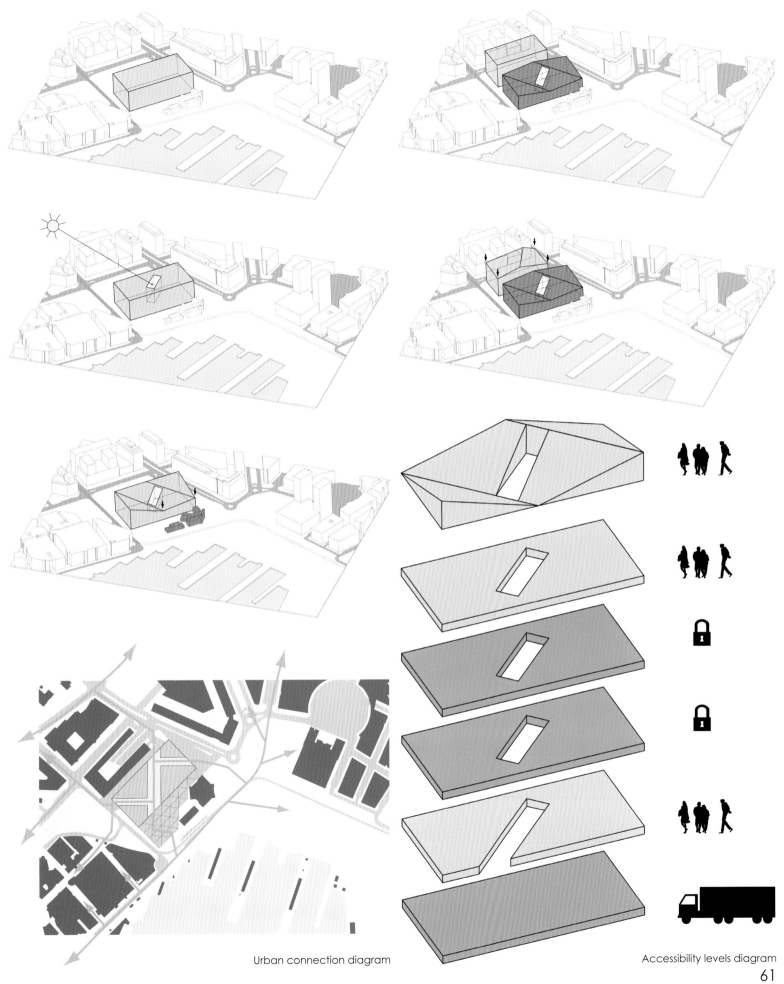

Urban connection diagram

Accessibility levels diagram

61

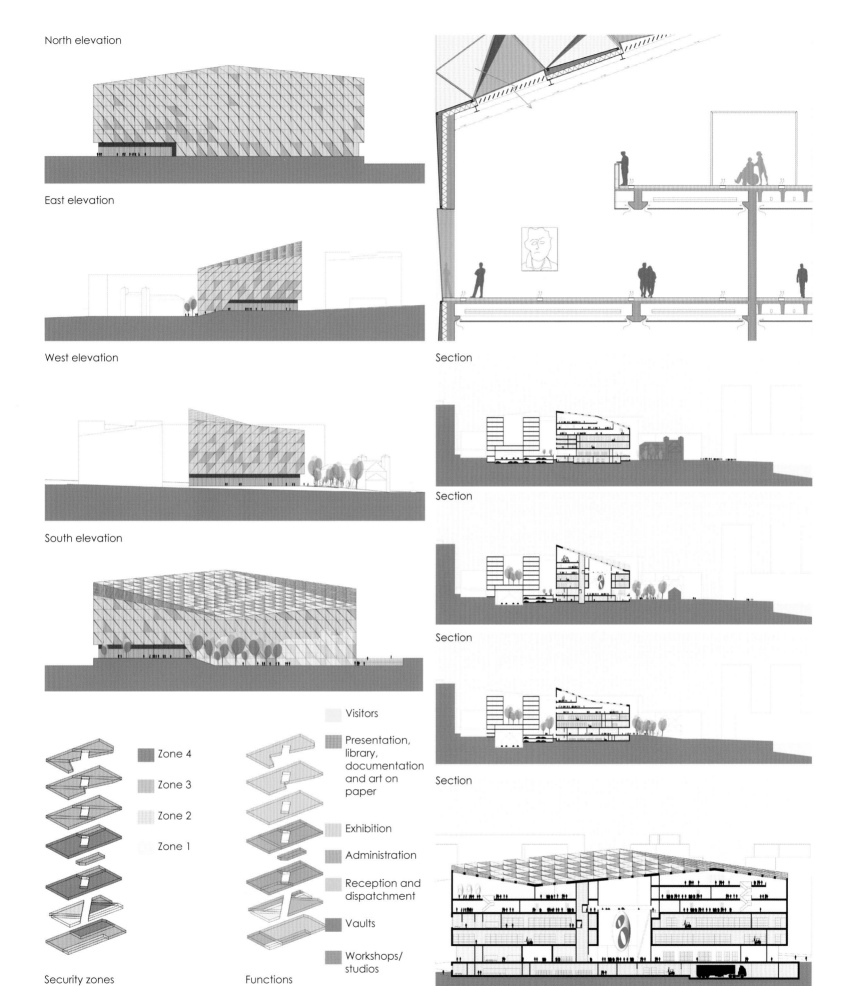

North elevation

East elevation

West elevation

Section

South elevation

Section

Section

Section

Security zones

Zone 4
Zone 3
Zone 2
Zone 1

Functions

Visitors
Presentation, library, documentation and art on paper
Exhibition
Administration
Reception and dispatchment
Vaults
Workshops/ studios

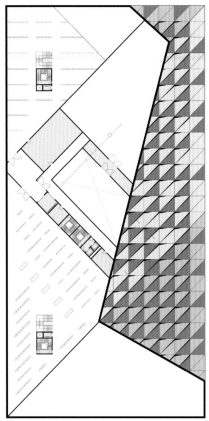

Seventh floor plan

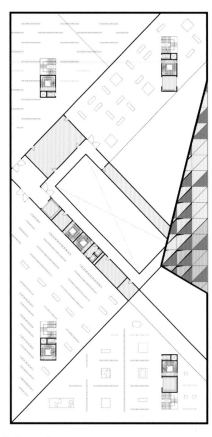

Sixth floor plan

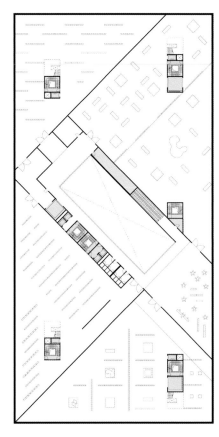

Fifth floor plan

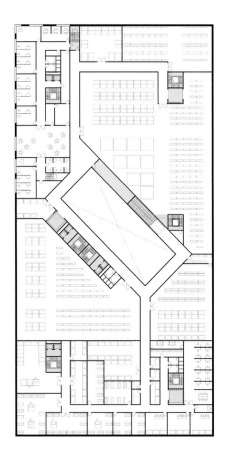

Fourth floor plan

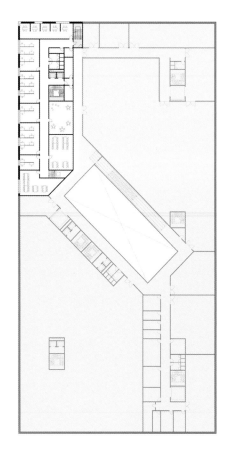

Third floor plan

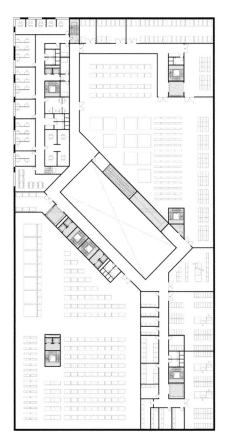

Second floor plan

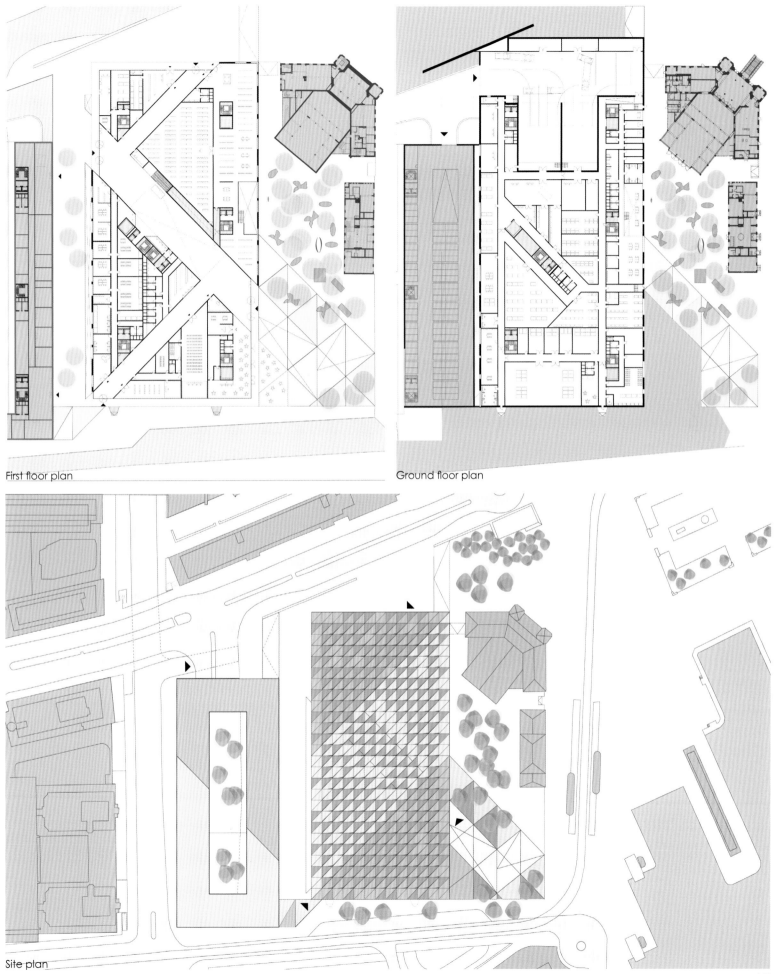

First floor plan

Ground floor plan

Site plan

65

Munch Museum

Location: Olso, Norway **Designer:** Herreros Arquitectos
Photographer: Jorge Queipo/Federico López
Competition Date: 2009 **Construction Area:** 16,000 sqm
Place in the Competition: 1st Prize

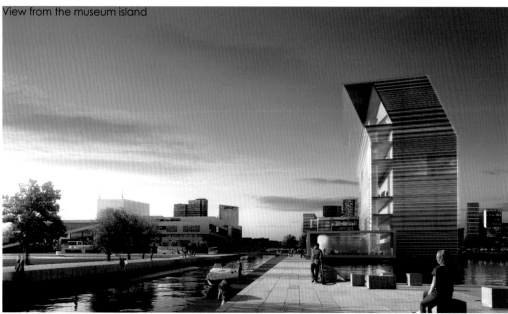

View from the museum island

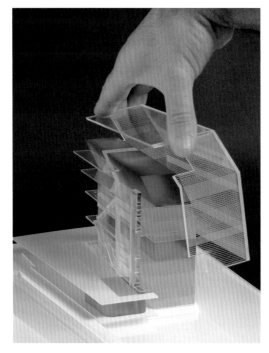

The Museum is conceived as an institution which is open to the city and highly visible, which must be visited many times in a lifetime because of its dynamic programmes but also because of its power as a place of concentration, walks and daily relaxation in its terraces and cafés or even because of its retail spaces.

The proposal as a whole is very notably involved with energy and environmental sensitivity issues. The detailed explanation of the operation of the Museum installations and its extension to the rest of the uses has been made clear. This is the moment to underscore the designers' firm position that these housing facilities, inasmuch as every other proposed building, not least Lambda's public spaces must adhere to the sustainable criteria hereby proposed, beginning with the very reduction of cost as first preventive measure.

View of mountain

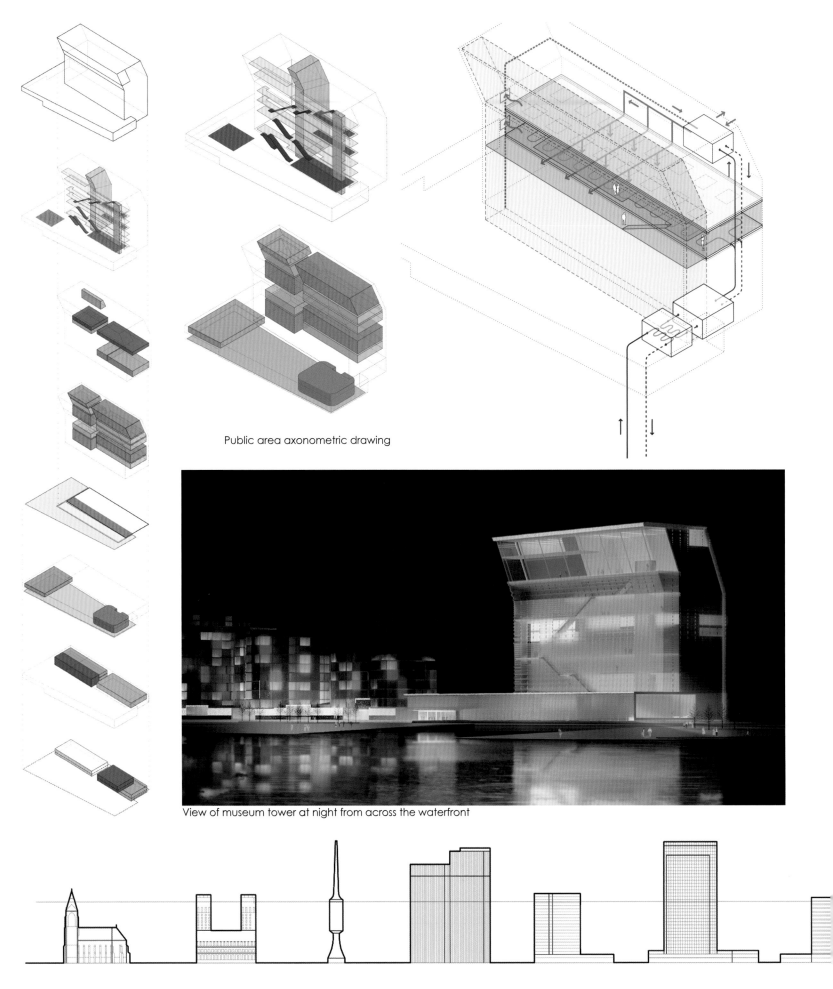

Public area axonometric drawing

View of museum tower at night from across the waterfront

View from the museum's water roof garden

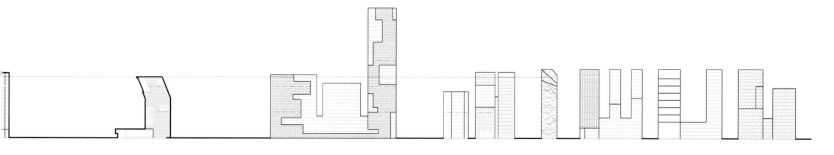

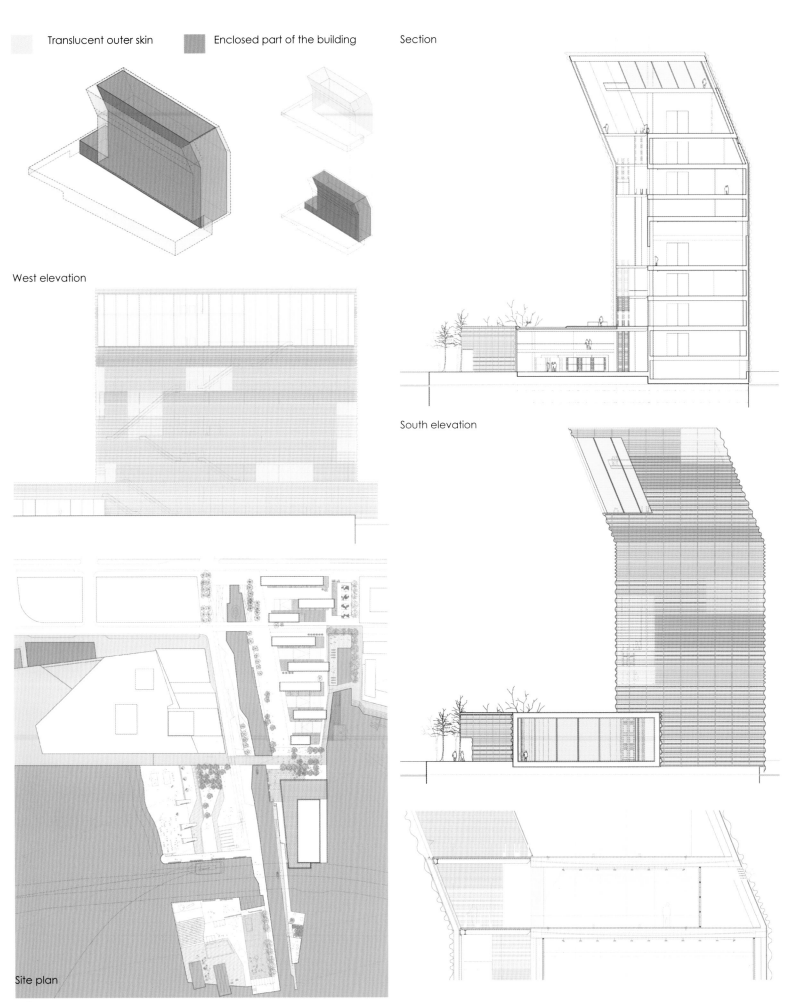

Translucent outer skin   Enclosed part of the building

Section

West elevation

South elevation

Site plan

70

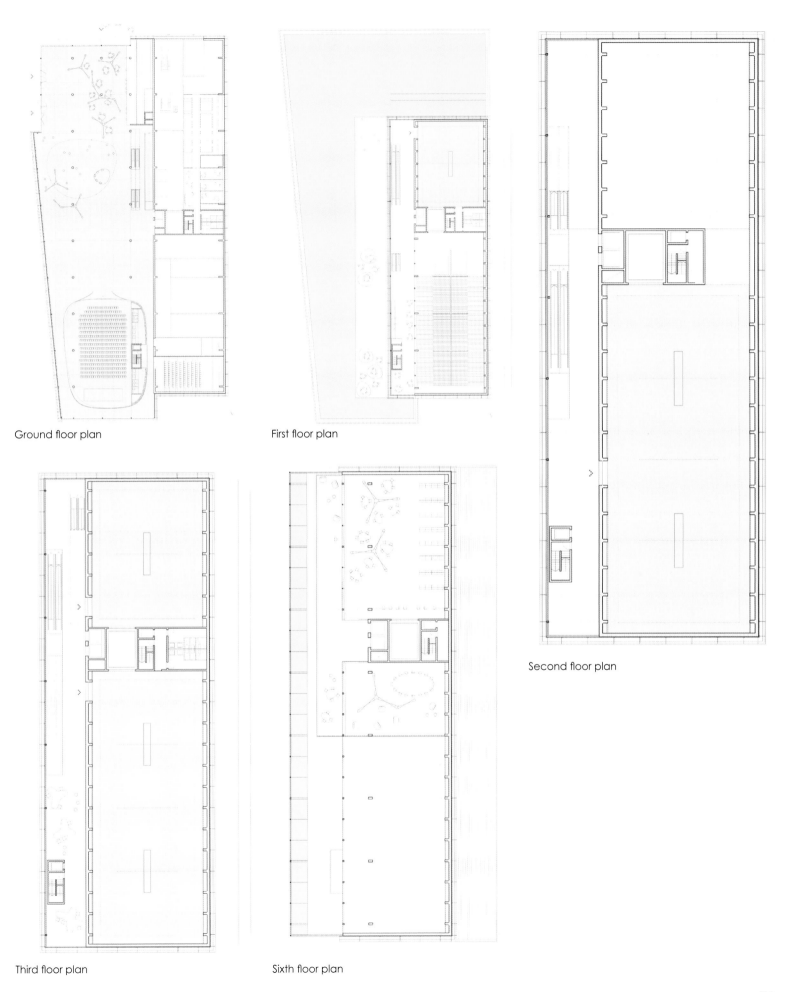

Ground floor plan

First floor plan

Second floor plan

Third floor plan

Sixth floor plan

Urban Transition

Location: Oslo, Norway **Designer:** JAJA Architects
Photographer: JAJA Architects, MIR VISUALS A/S
Competition Date: 2009 **Competition Name:** International
Competition for National Museum of Art, Architecture
and Design in Oslo, Norway **Site Area:** 70,000 sqm **Place
in the Competition:** 2nd Prize

Awarded reason:
The strength of Urban Transition is the proposal's
composition and its links to the surrounding
city. The volumes are successful in breaking
up the large dimensions. The composition and
adaptation to the surroundings are elegant –
the composition creates an outstanding depth
from the shore side.

The proposal's main concept is a Kasimple
composition of five rectangular buildings linked
by light glass buildings. The five buildings are
individually scaled to match their immediate
surroundings, from the low cornice height of
the Vestbane buildings to the high gables
of Munkedamsveien. The government office
building is included as a six-storey block facing
Munkedamsveien, situated so as to form a square
between the office building and the museum.
The project relates well to cultural heritage
buildings and neighbouring buildings. The
project has a thorough and well-considered
environmental strategy. The energy concept
is mainly based on constructional/passive
measures, and building volumes are compact.
It is estimated that the project could fulfill the
goals for use of resources, substances hazardous
to health and the environment, lifespan and low
greenhouse gas emissions.

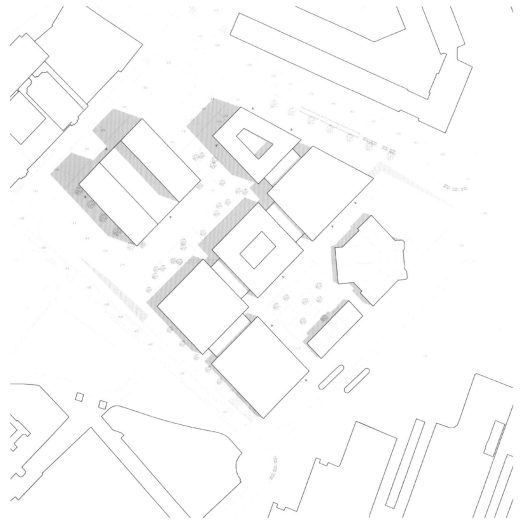

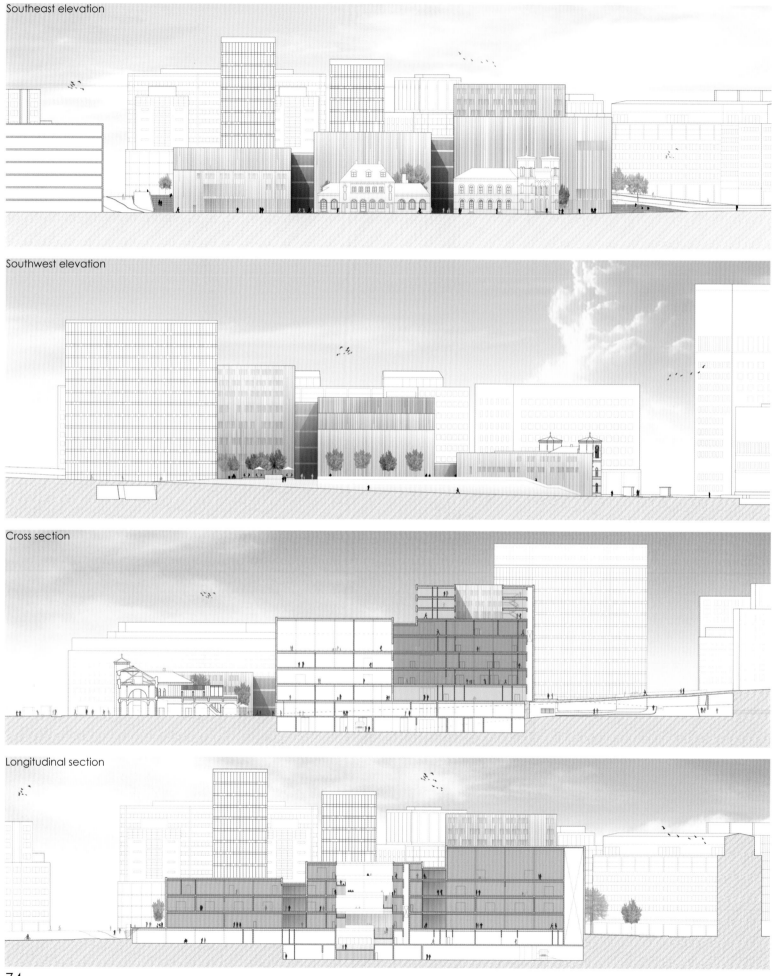

Southeast elevation

Southwest elevation

Cross section

Longitudinal section

74

Waterside

Town hall

Overview

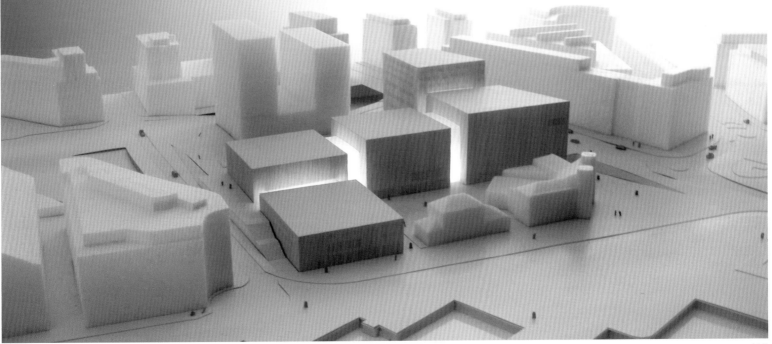

View of the square

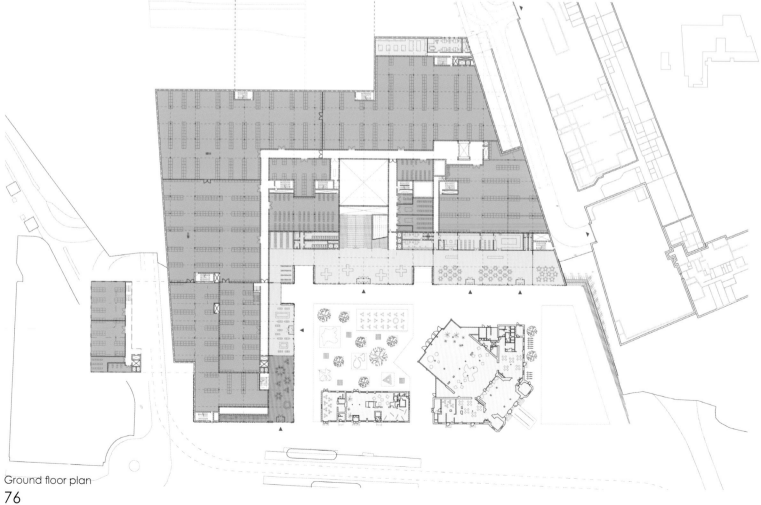

Ground floor plan

Lobby

Separation scale

3SOME

Location: Oslo, Norway **Designer:** LABSCAPE Architecture
Photographer: LABSCAPE Architecture **Competition Date:** 2009 **Competition Name:** Competition for National Museum for Art, Design and Architecture, Oslo, Norway
Construction Area: 74, 840 sqm **Place in the Competition:** Entry

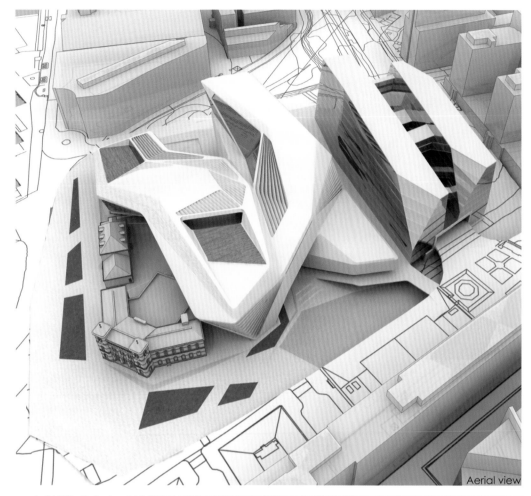

Aerial view

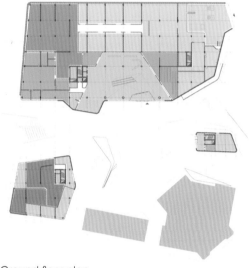

Ground floor plan

The Museum uses its twisted geometry standing on the massive footing to introduce series of event spaces, from landscape to interior exhibition to roofscape, nesting all aspects of art experiences in one move.

Inside the Museum the exhibitions are linked horizontally and vertically to form a continuous spiral. Formation of the geometry starts from first situating the strong movement of the massing. This geometry then provides the common logic for further articulation such as carved spaces or inlaid openings as a synthetic body. The technology came in the form of self-compacting concrete in which chemical additives are introduced into the concrete mix, significantly increasing its workability without any resultant loss in strength.

The project is conceived like a bridge. Sustainable design integrates environmental, economic, and social issues of sustainability together with users' goals and needs. The NMAAD Museum employs sustainable design to reduce energy consumption, reduce greenhouse gas emissions, encourage water conservation, and provide high indoor environmental quality.

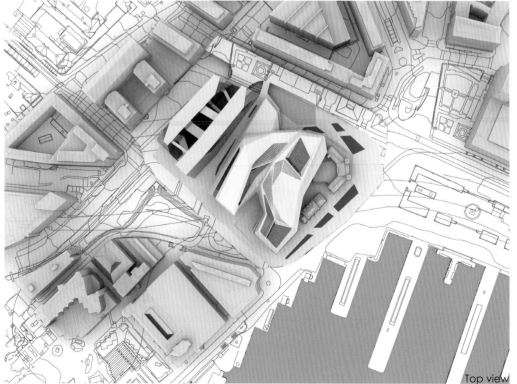

Top view

General view

Access from Enga Street

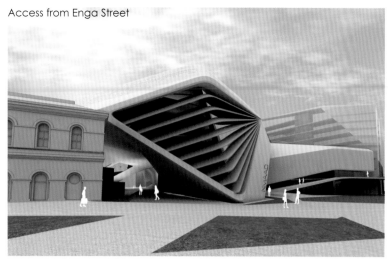

Access from Dokkveien

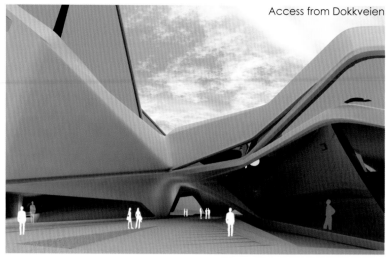

Access from Radhusbrgge

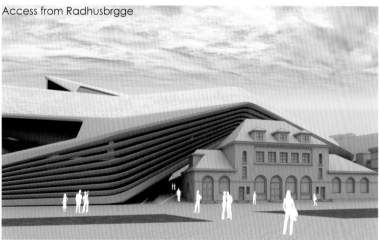

Access from Nobel Peace Centre

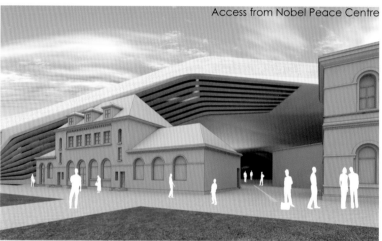

Entrance of the museum from Art Plaza

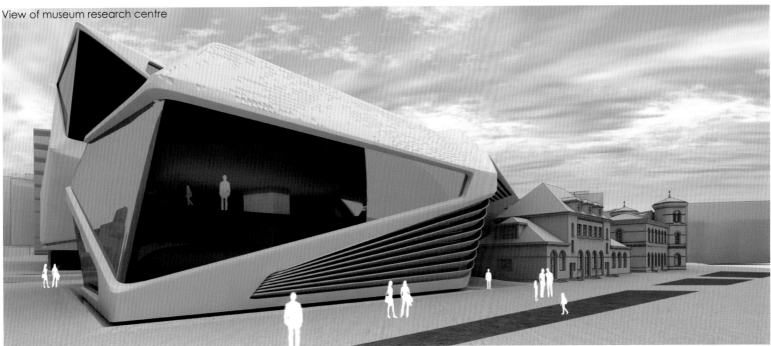
View of museum research centre

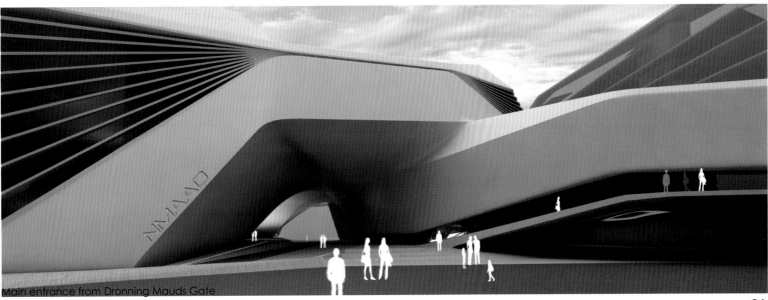
Main entrance from Dronning Mauds Gate

Lobby of the museum

Concept

Section AA

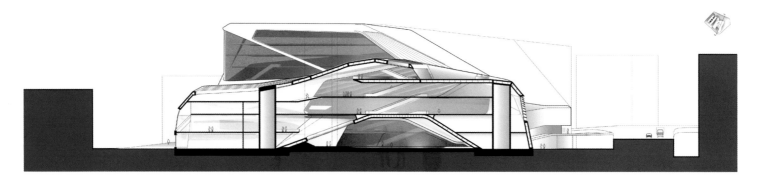

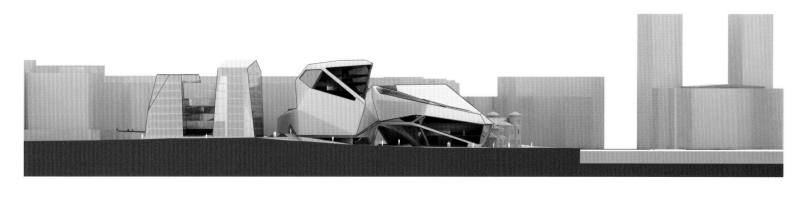

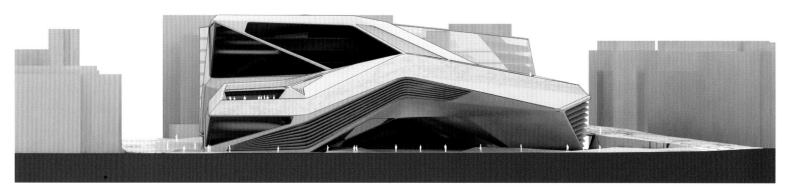

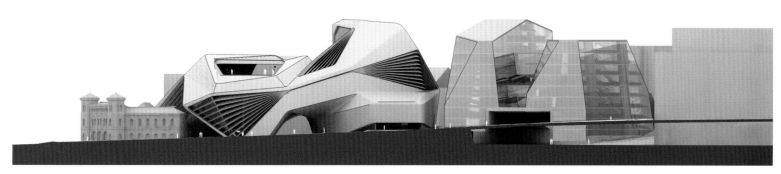

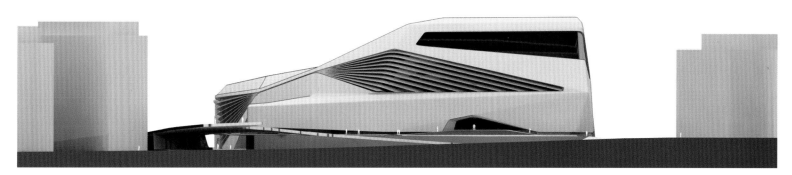

Section BB

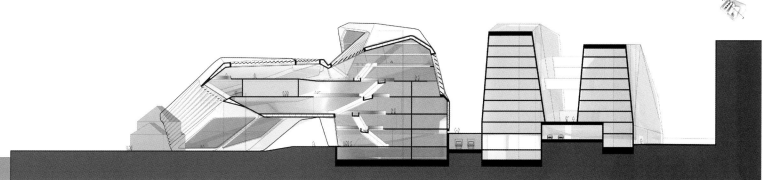

Museum plan

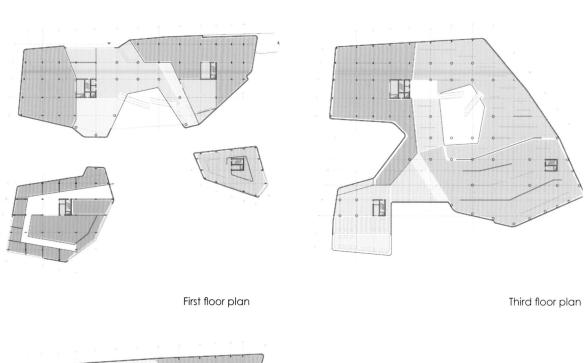

First floor plan

Third floor plan

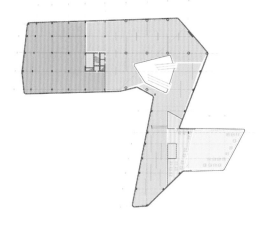

Second floor plan

Fourth floor plan

Office floor plan

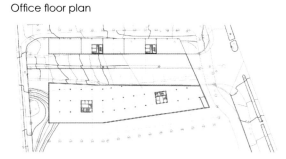

Ground level

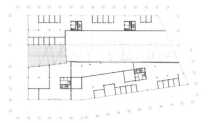

Level 01

Level 03

Lower ground level

Level 02

Level 04

84

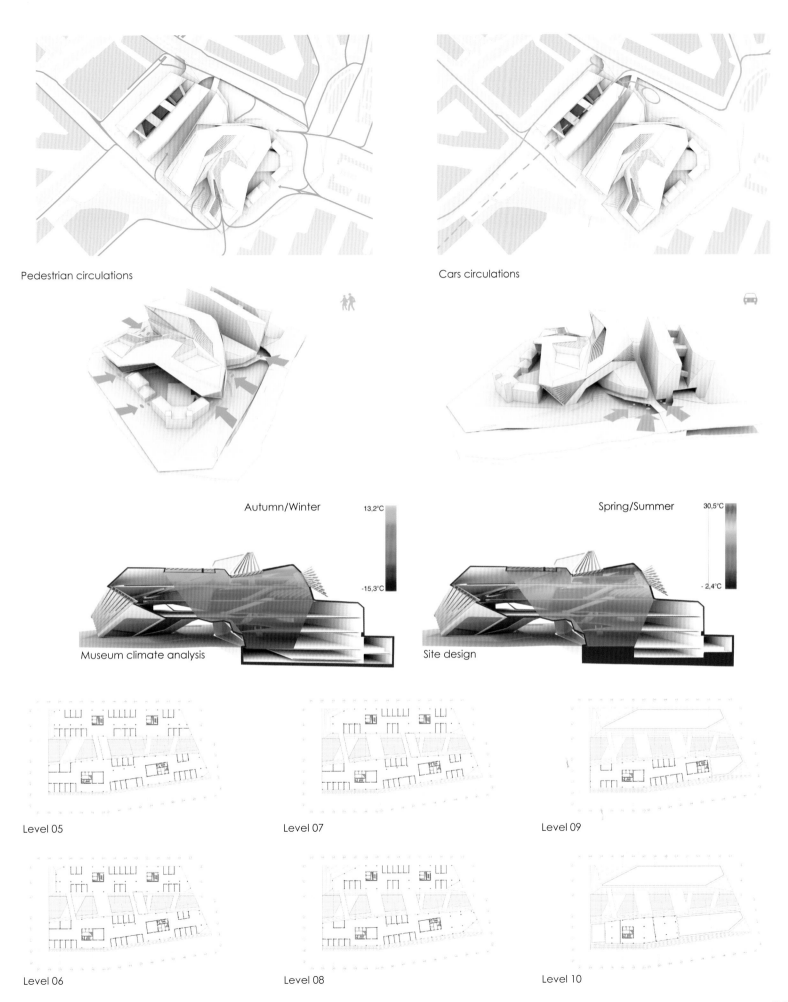

Pedestrian circulations

Cars circulations

Autumn/Winter   13,2°C

-15,3°C

Museum climate analysis

Spring/Summer   30,5°C

- 2,4°C

Site design

Level 05

Level 07

Level 09

Level 06

Level 08

Level 10

Rainwater harvesting

Spring / Summer

Photovoltaic cells

Autumn/Winter

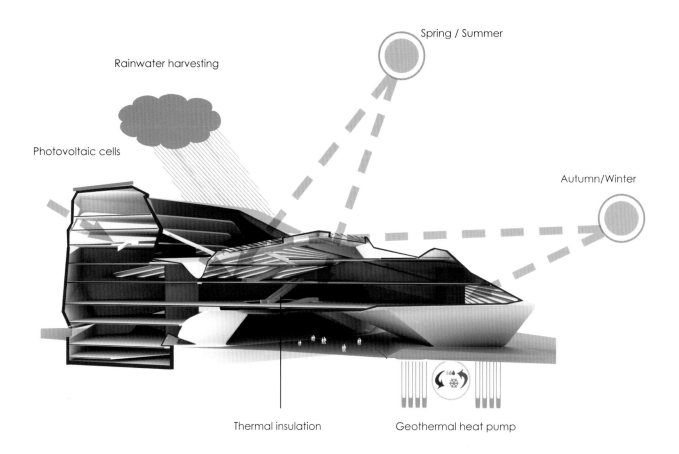

Thermal insulation

Geothermal heat pump

Interior circulation diagram

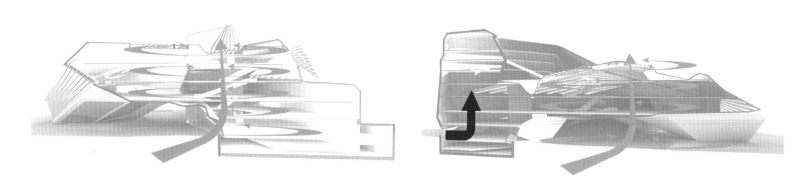

The whole circulation is based on a fluid circulation that leads you peacefully
through the museum

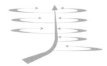

Museum primary circulation

Museum secondary circulation

Office circulation

Museum primary circulation

Programme diagrams

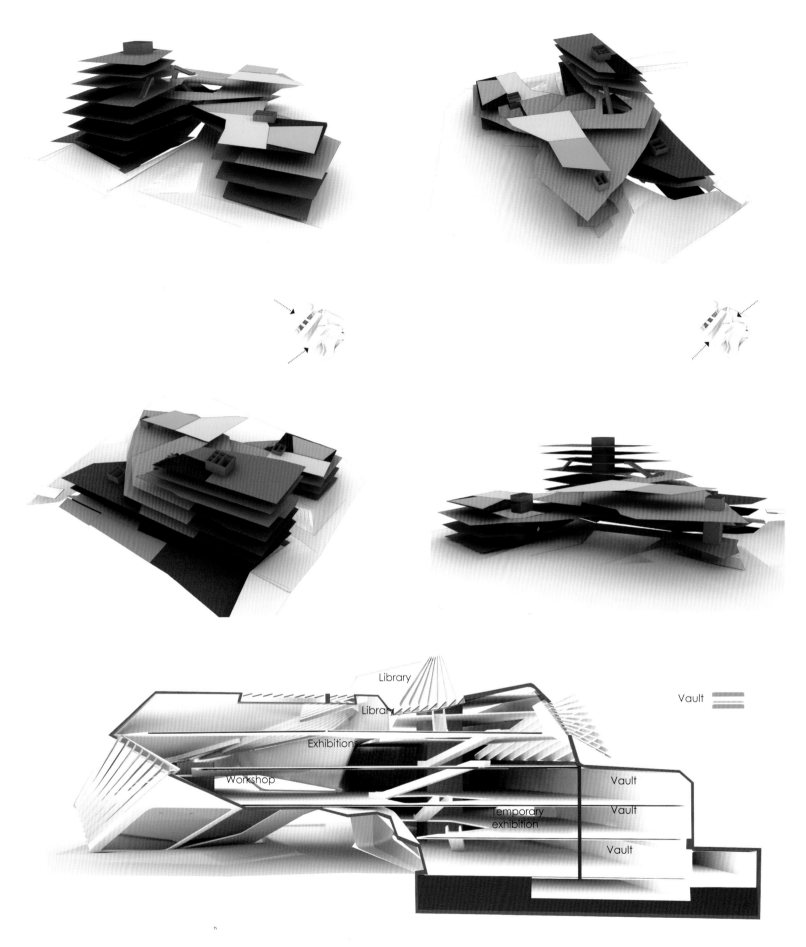

Library

Library

Exhibitions

Workshop

Vault

Temporary
exhibition

Vault

Vault

Vault

Back in Black

Location: Oslo, Norway **Designer:** Rodeo arkitekter
Competition Date: 2009 **Competition Name:** International
Competition for National Museum for Art, Design and
Architecture, Oslo, Norway **Site Area:** 5,000 sqm **Place
in the Competition:** Shortlist

Awarded reason:
It is the designers' opinion that a national
museum, with its public programmes, needs to
open up not only to the public, but also to the
city structure, becoming the urban connector this
part of Oslo sorely needs.

The National Museum contains four core
programmes: Exhibition Spaces, Storage
Vaults and Conservation, Library, Learning and
Presentation, Administration and Management.
By separating the programmes the designers are
able to make clear what the National Museum
consists of. It also allows for individual approaches
to building design, architectural expression, and
a placement of functions that better correspond
with the highly varied programmes requirements.
Splitting up the project into smaller units also
allows for a more gentle approach to the site,
on a scale that relates better to the existing
Vestbane buildings.
The project holds high ambitions with regards
to environmental sustainability. Focus areas are
low carbon gas emission, energy efficiency,
sustainable materials and robust technical
solutions. The museum building qualifies as a
"Class A Building" according to Norwegian energy
classifications. The simple palette of materials,
Larvikitt (dark stone), and recycled glass reduces
the building's CO_2 emission dramatically. The
roofs are covered with sedum (stonecrop) in
different shades. The sedum has a positive effect
on the local environment in an urban setting like
this.

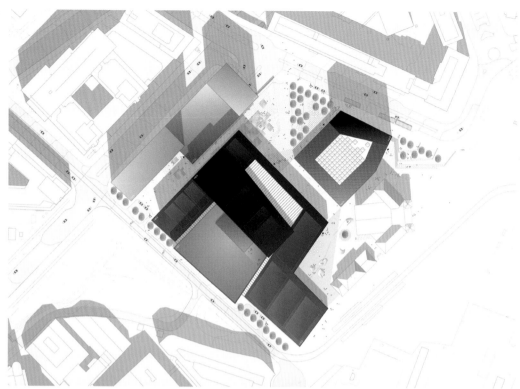

Bird's-eye view at night

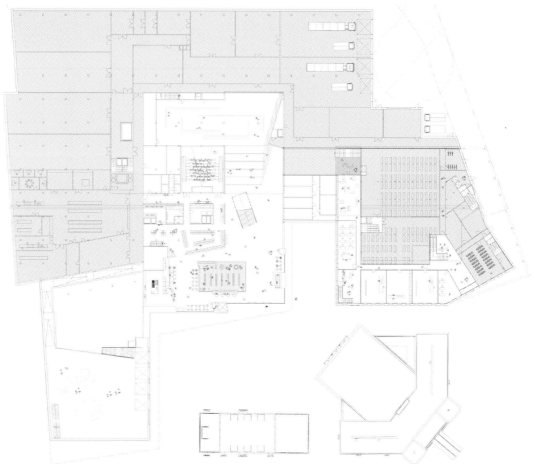

First floor plan

Entrance lower plaza

 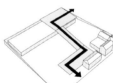 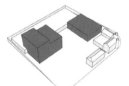   

Interior exhibition

Section

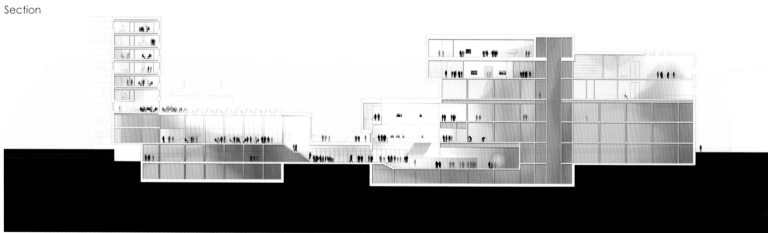

Southeast elevation

92

Front view at night

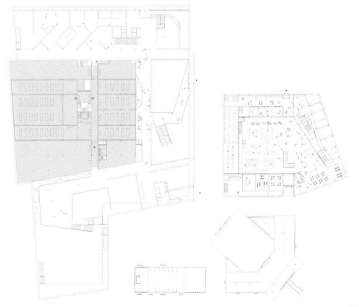

Ground floor plan

Taiyuan Museum of Art

Location: Taiyuan, China **Designer:** Preston Scott Cohen, Inc. **Competition Date:** 2007 **Competition Name:** Taiyuan Museum of Art International Competition **Construction Area:** 40,500 sqm **Place in the Competition:** 1st Prize

Awarded reason:
The building's strong dynamic form is a geometric spin on the agricultural landscapes native to the Shanxi Province. The tessellated surfaces respond to contemporary technologies for controlling natural and artificial light, in addition to producing unexpected spatial conditions as the user circulates through and around the building.

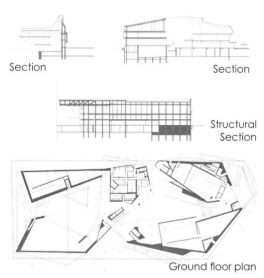

Section

Section

Structural Section

Ground floor plan

The museum is a cluster of buildings unified by a dialectic of continuity and discontinuity. The building produces the impression of a continuous sequence of spaces while at the same time giving visitors the freedom either to follow a chronological sequence or to skip from one cluster of galleries to another, in a non-linear fashion. An exterior ramp threading through the building connects the heterogeneous hardscapes, lawns and sculpture gardens. The integration of building and landscape registers multiple scales of territory ranging from the enormity of the Fen River to the intimacy of the museum's own particular spatial episodes. Inside, the security of museum space is maintained by a highly controlled interface between gallery and non-gallery programmes. The individual sets of lifts and cores are distributed to guarantee easy access and divisibility between zones regulated by different schedules and rules of access.

Entrance view

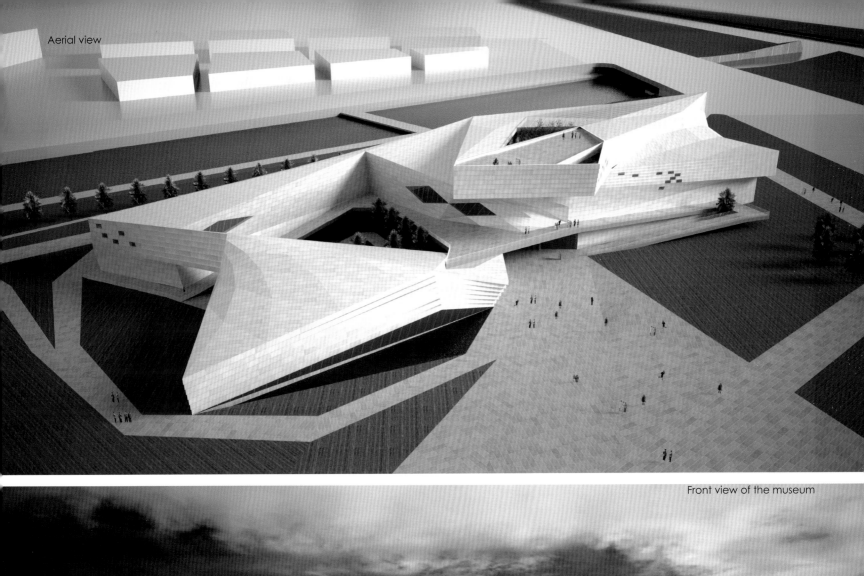
Aerial view

Front view of the museum

Atrium

Elevations

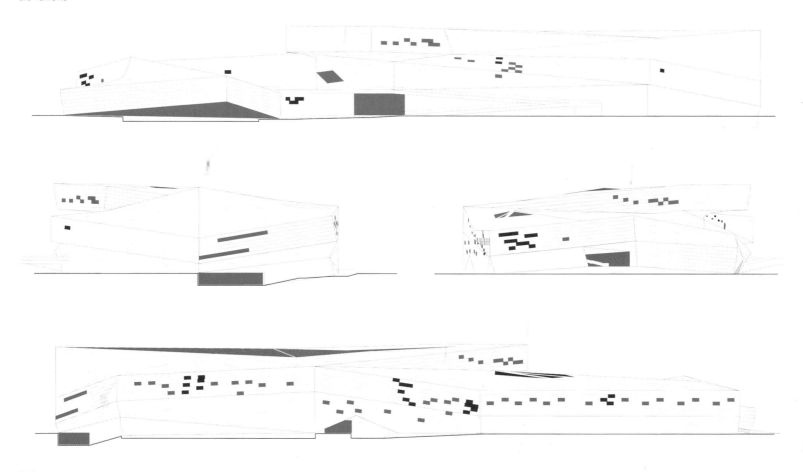

Gallery space

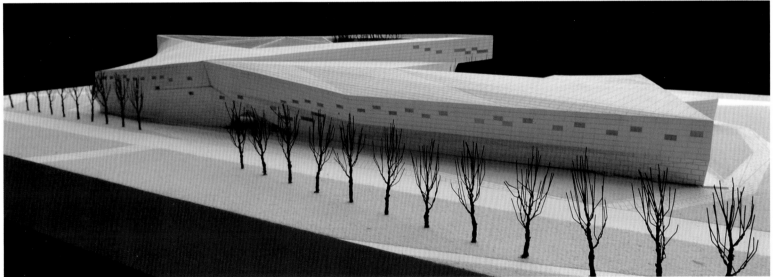

Courtyard

Sprengel Museum Extension

Location: Hannover, Germany **Designer:** LAN Architecture **Competition Date:** 2010 **Competition Name:** Sprengel Museum Extension International Competition **Construction Area:** 4,200 sqm **Place in the Competition:** Entry

Awarded reason:
The proposal seeks to create interaction between the museum site and its immediate surroundings, between a building and a topography.

Perspective

The project's verticality enables responses to all the project's challenges in a single gesture: the connection and enhancement of the plinth, the institution's visibility, the renewal of its image, the creation of diverse and flexible exhibition spaces, a dialogue with the existing architecture. The museum announces its presence to the city whilst enabling the landscape of the lake and the city, the spaces it seeks to embrace, to penetrate within its confines.

The vertical configuration, structured by the stacking and staggering of its component spaces provides an enormous possibility for modularity and flexibility: When closed, these volumes become pure "white cubes", the classic conceptual exhibition space. When staggered, they open up intermediate rest spaces between the exhibition rooms, bathed in natural light. Balconies looking out over the cityscape act as havens of rest, and become an integral part of the visitor's itinerary through the museum. When open, the exhibition spaces create a dialogue between the works inside and the cityscape they reflect.

Night view

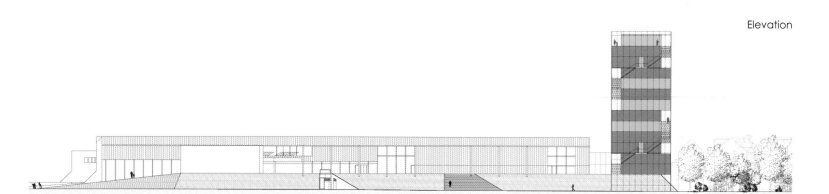

Elevation

Open hall

View of balcony

100

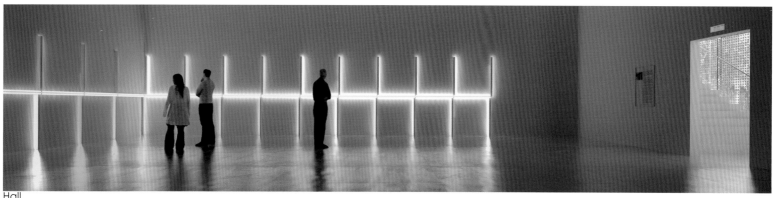

Hall

Roof floor

Stairway

Fine Arts Museum Nantes

Location: Nantes, France **Designer:** Manuelle Gautrand **Photographer:** Platform, Manuelle Gautrand Architecture, Arthur Couprie **Competition Date:** 2009 **Competition Name:** Fine Art Museum in Nantes, France, Competition **Construction Area:** 17,000 sqm **Place in the Competition:** 2nd Prize

Awarded reason:
The whole project becomes an urban strategy, developing several new façades around the block, beginning to be very attractive at the town's scale.

The museum of fine arts, located in Nantes, has a big objective of refurbishment and extension. In terms of functionalities, the entrance was small, and its connections with the other facilities (café, auditorium, library and temporary exhibitions) are actually very difficult to find. The designers have decided to move the lobby and all the facilities in a very vast lower level, located under the ground floor.

The main advantage is to keep the existing XIX museum in a respectful refurbishment, which doesn't touch and doesn't alter the historical aspect. The other one is to create a generous and fluid space, bringing together all the common functions. The two extended parts are mainly dedicated to exhibit the contemporary art. Two envelops are created: the first one is a glass wall and the secondary, fixed on the exterior side, is made with long strips which are weaved together. It's like a wicker basket: The long prefabricated concrete strips are crossing together diagonally, in a progressive way. The strips are going smaller, giving more natural light in the high levels. All the new architecture, extended building and public spaces are made with a beige concrete, mimicking the specific stone of Nantes.

View from the street Georges Clemenceau

Night view

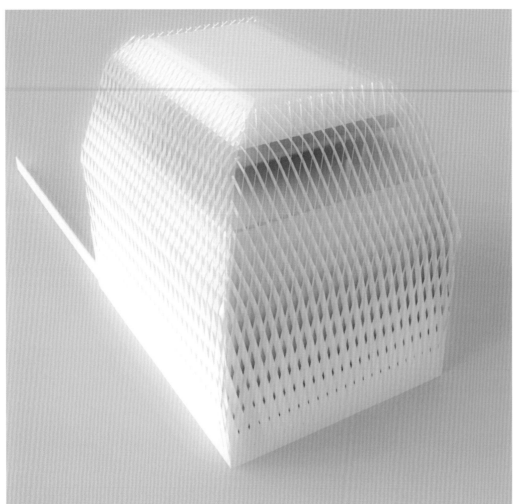

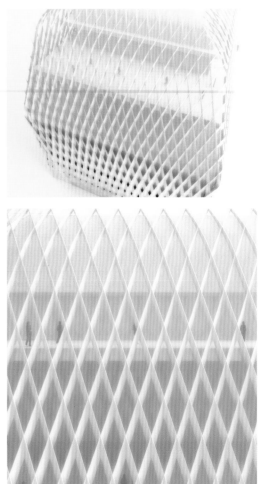

Garden lining the building

The hall

Fine arts gallery

Modern art gallery

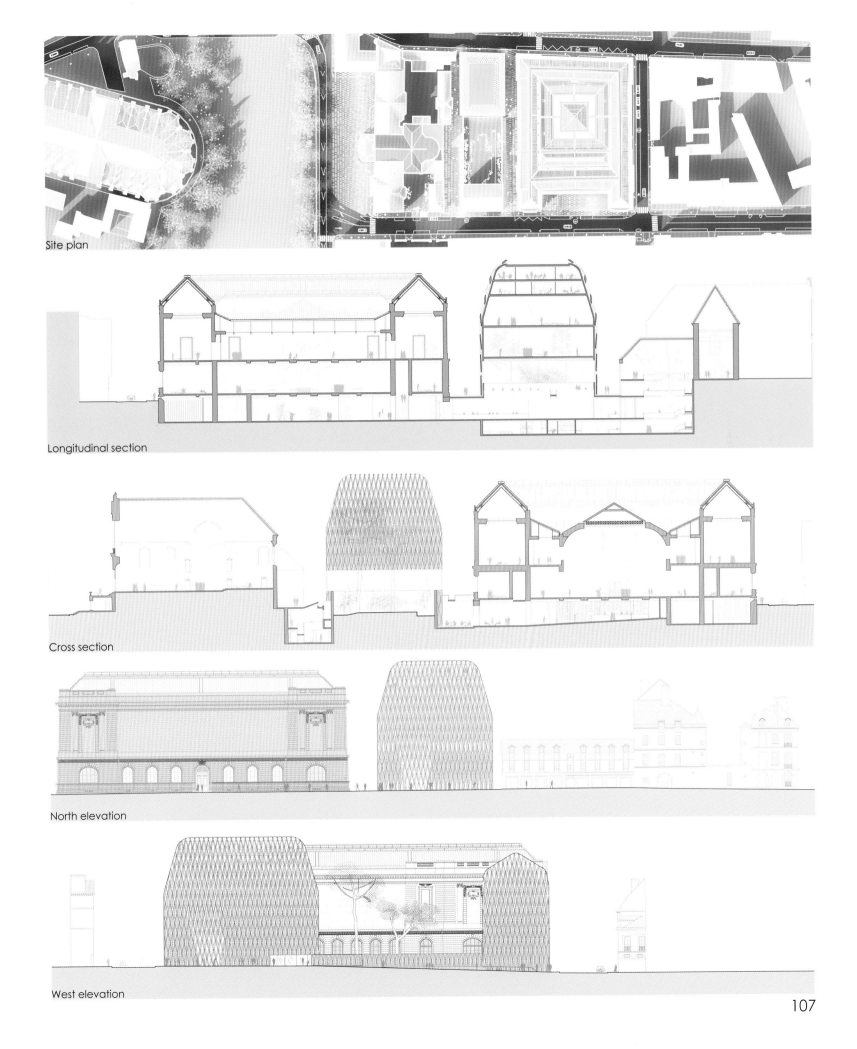

Site plan

Longitudinal section

Cross section

North elevation

West elevation

Kunst Museum Basel

Location: Basel, Switzerland **Designer:** Alejandro Aravena/ELEMENTAL **Photographer:** ELEMENTAL **Competition Date:** 2008 **Site Area:** 10,580 sqm

The museum is in one of the most prominent city openings, with five streets coming together, one of them actually a bridge so wide and with such long views that it is, in a sense, a public space in itself.

So, how do the designers participate in that potential hierarchy by improving the opening but not loose valuable well-located land necessary for the museum? The proposal is to contribute to the hierarchy of this place by liberating as much space as possible on the ground level and reorienting the upper volumes in a strategic way. At the pedestrian level, buildings cantilever to allow diagonals and shortcuts to create both more direct connections and longer views. On upper levels, façades are reoriented to take advantage of this newly acquired scale, particularly the one whose north orientation can open towards the bridge and the river.

Foyer

Entrance

Foyer

Ground floor plan

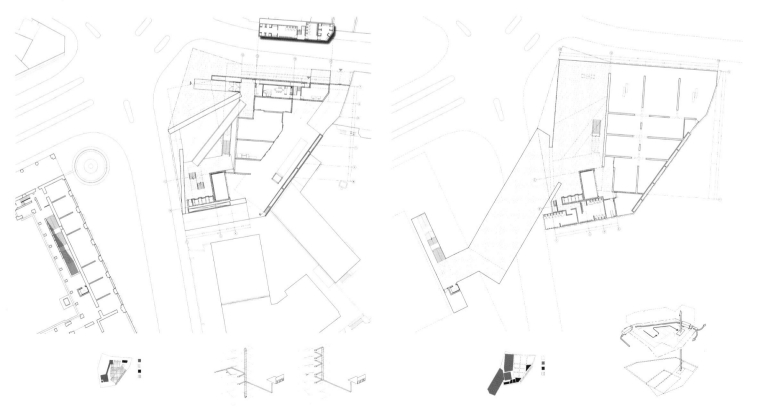

Gallery space

Tower

112

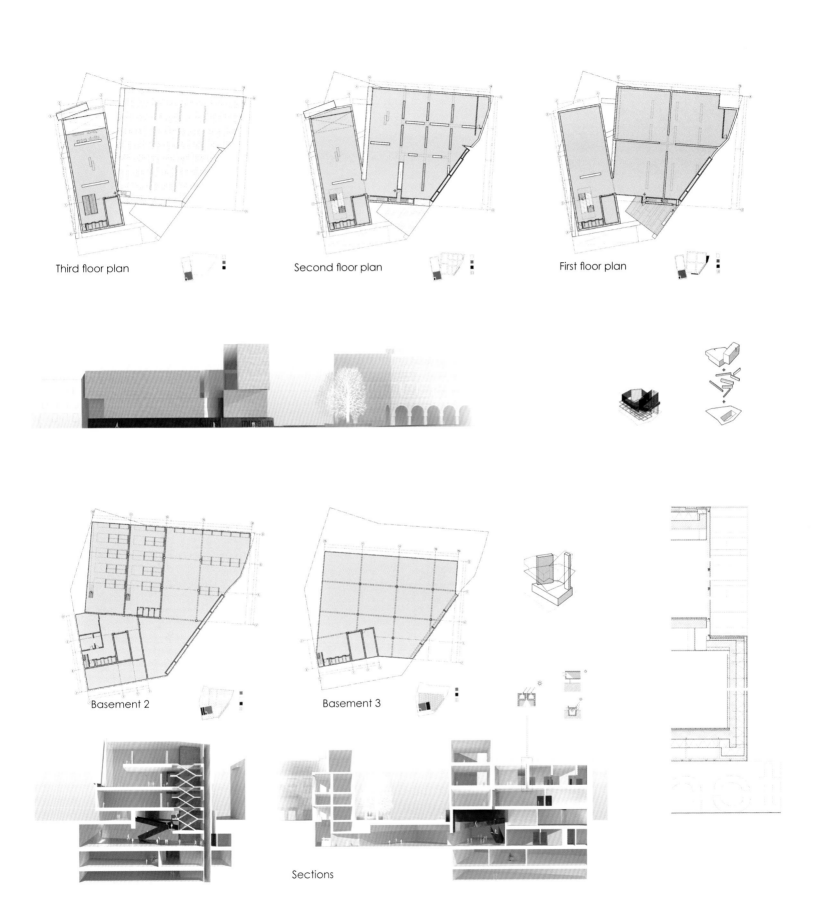

Third floor plan

Second floor plan

First floor plan

Basement 2

Basement 3

Sections

Museum of Modern Art in Medellin

Location: Medellin, Colombia **Designer:** Alejandro Aravena/ELEMENTAL **Photographer:** ELEMENTAL **Competition date:** 2009 **Site area:** 4,200 sqm

A museum is a building over the city, a special item. The works that are exhibited here, are not the simple example of an artistic production average, but represent an outstanding example of what a society is able to create. It is the uniqueness of the institution (museum) and production (art), the container and contents, which converges to the city and the community around a museum. Therefore the designers propose a roundabout way, which leaves a strong mark in the city and its citizens.

Each time you work in a building complex, new items must find a way to be understood as part of the place that welcomes them. The designers propose two materials to build links with both the overall and the neighbourhood: First base the proposal on the use of brick, a noble material, old and rich, one could say, almost scenery. Secondly the designers propose the concrete, which not only creates a continuity with the existing building, but also creates a neutral background against which the main element can be appreciated.

Façade of the museum

Overview

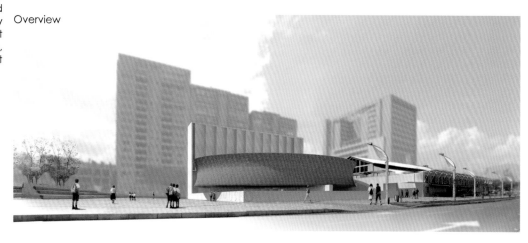

Section

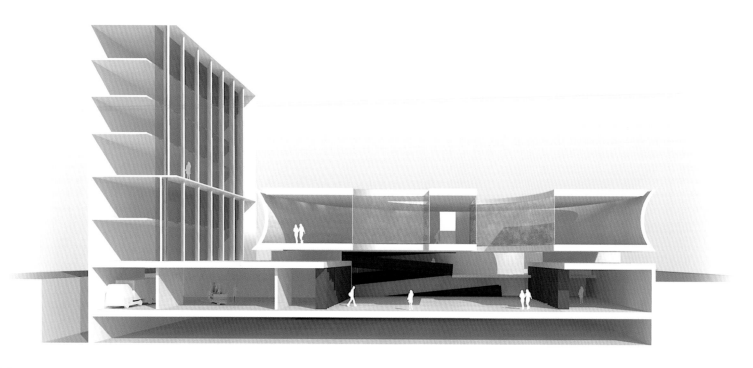

Exhibition space

General view

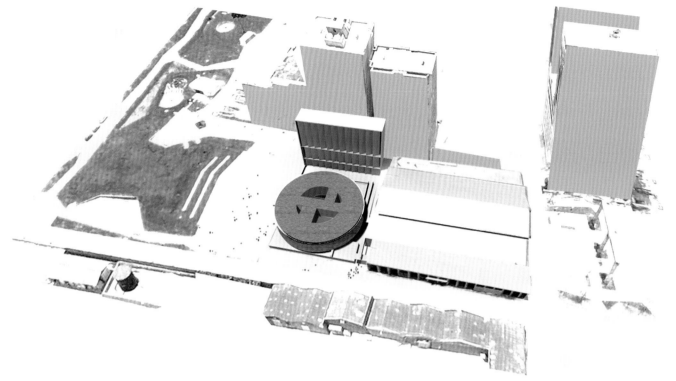

Plans

Skyline Rooftop Museum

Location: Maribor, Slovenia **Designer:** OFIS Architect **Competition Date:** 2010 **Competition Name:** Competition for Museum of Modern Art Maribor **Construction Area:** 40,000 sqm **Place in the Competition:** Finalist

The building is placed within the forecast area in a way that establishes a dialogue with its surroundings and respects the existing volumes and flows. The volume of the complex is a synthesis of the major orthogonal cubes and the finest triangulated structures. In a symbolic way it represents a synthesis of new build cubes at the western side of the site and the fragmented tissue that is created by historical pitched roof buildings on the west. The proposed volume softens and creates a visual transition between the historical and new.

Functional volumes are main large programmatic units (exhibition space, lecture hall, library...), and triangulated structures are light boxes that guide the northern lights, and partly also create space for programmes with lower heights. Mixture of volumes and structures is creating dynamics and communicative ambient inside and outside of the building. It creates terraces and patios at different levels and mix of external and internal space.

View to the lobby from the first floor balcony bridge

Towards the museum entrance

View from the old Maribor bridge

Museum lobby

Towards the permanent exhibition on the first floor

Contemporary exhibition on the second floor

Museum in between river bank and old part Maribor skyline

Elevation view from the opposite river bank

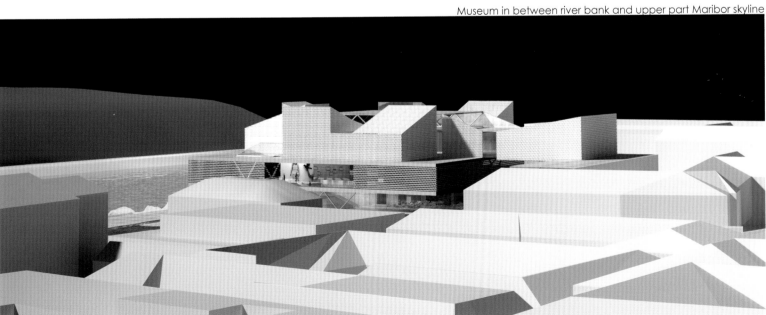
Museum in between river bank and upper part Maribor skyline

123

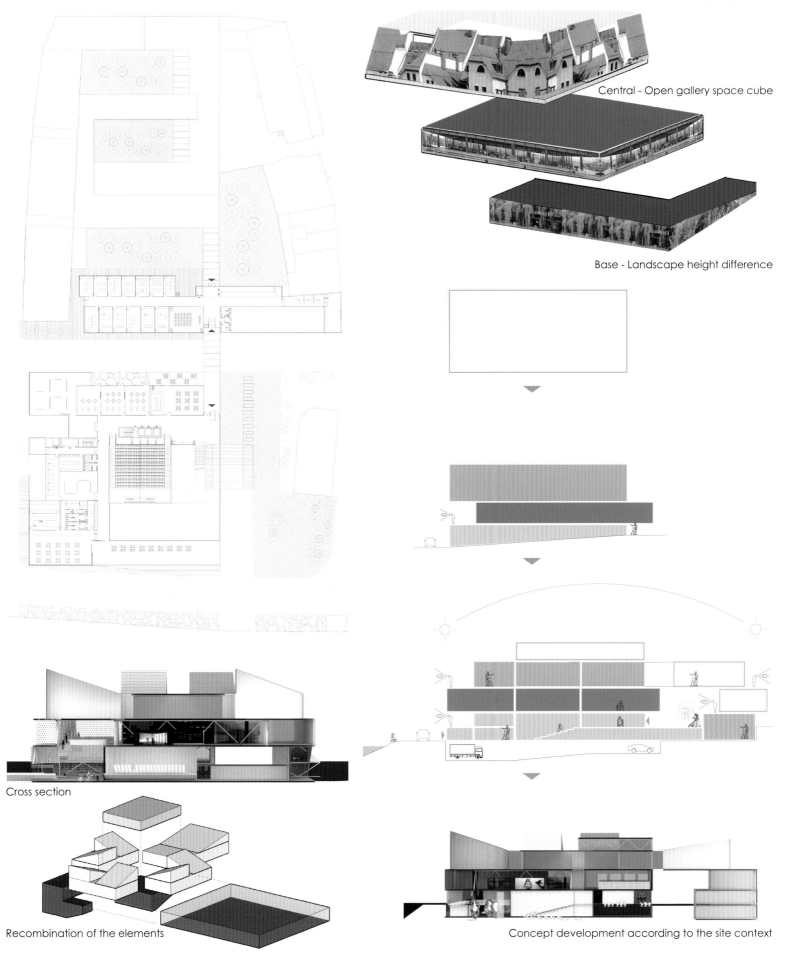

Ground floor plan

City skyline - Roof tops gallery spaces

Central - Open gallery space cube

Base - Landscape height difference

Cross section

Recombination of the elements

Concept development according to the site context

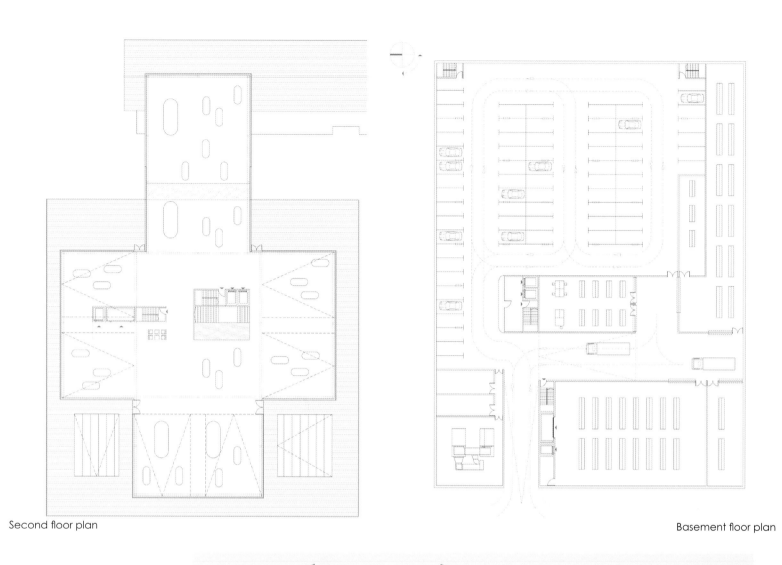

Second floor plan

Basement floor plan

Third floor plan

Longitudinal section

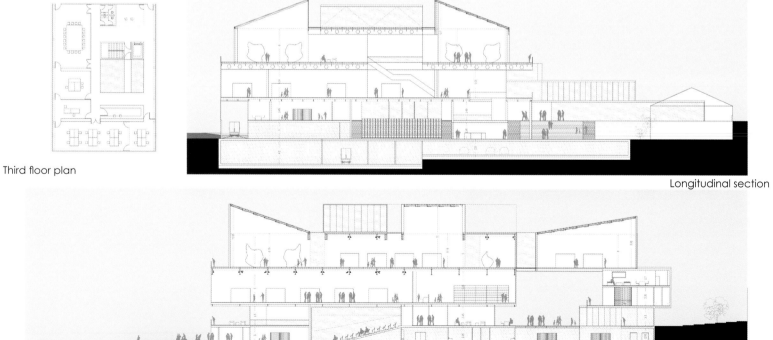

Cross section

First floor plan

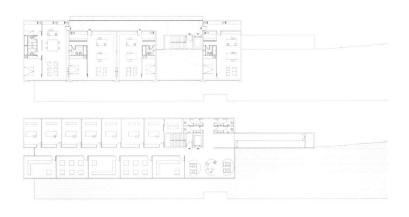

Floor4
Floor3
Floor2
Floor1
Floor0
Floor-1

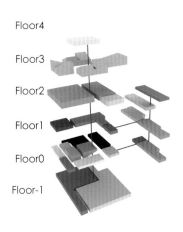

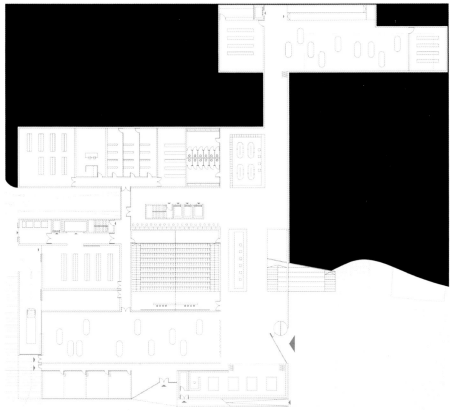

Temporary exhibition area

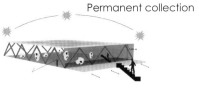

Permanent collection

Temporary exhibition area

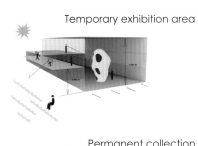

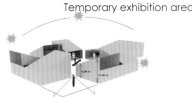

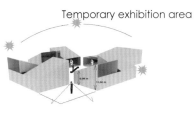

Lower ground

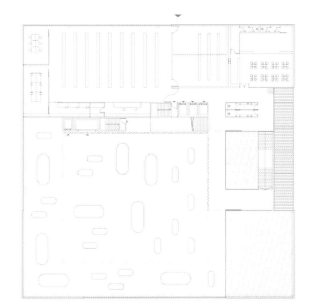

First floor plan

East elevation

West elevation

North elevation

South elevation

127

Danish Maritime Museum

Location: Helsingor, Denmark **Designer:** BIG **Competition Date:** 2008 **Competition Name:** Contest to Design the New "Danish Maritime Museum" **Site Area:** 5,000 sqm **Place in the Competition:** 1st Prize

Awarded reason:
Designed to respect its immediate environment, the museum is placed around the dock and not inside it. This preserves the dock as an empty space to be used for outdoor activities, exhibitions and events. A number of footbridges cross over the dock create a dynamic tension.

General view

In order to build the Maritime Museum in the old dry dock it had to be reinforced in order not to cave in. The designers could either support the structure through an added layer of concrete throughout its interior but this would cover its beautiful old concrete walls or by digging around the dry dock walls and creating supportive rib walls on its exterior which proves to be too costly. Instead they propose to bend the rules of the competition and place the museum on the periphery of the dry dock walls in order to both act as its new reinforcing structure but also serving as the façade of the new museum.

The museum is actually one continuous ramp performing a loop around the dry dock walls. Three bridges provide easy access across the void and connect different galleries with one another, to the main entrance and Helsingor's harbour beyond. The continuous ramp's gentle slope is a minor 1/50 which corresponds to water running off a bathroom floor, a public square or a ships deck.

Tunnels

Entrance plaza

Basement 2

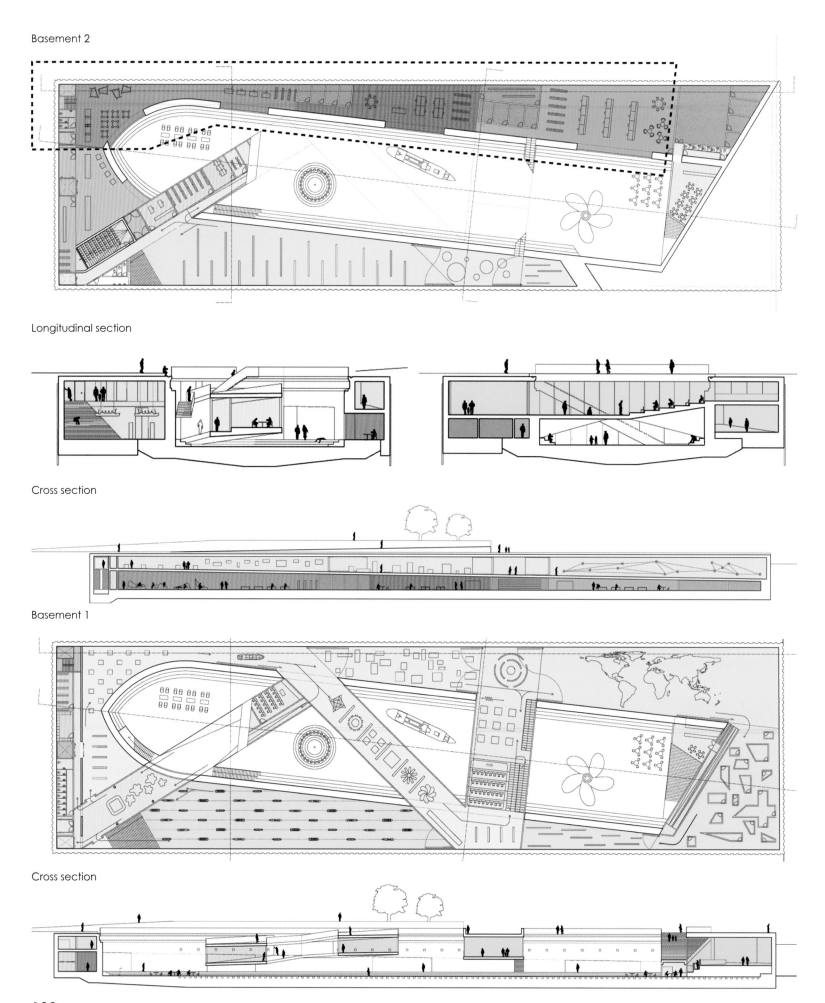

Longitudinal section

Cross section

Basement 1

Cross section

Exhibition spaces

Exhibition spaces

Exhibition spaces

Shanghai Natural History Museum

Entry from southeast

Location: Shanghai, China **Designer:** Perkins+Will
Competition Date: 2010 **Site Area:** 12,092 sqm
Construction Area: 45,086 sqm **Place in the Competition:**
1st Prize

The museum sits on an urban site, adjacent to a proposed sculpture park. The shape and internal organisation of the building are inspired by the form of the nautilus shell. A spiraling landscaped plane rises out of the sculpture park and wraps around an oval pond. The pond is the central visual focus of the exhibition route through the building, which begins at the upper level and spirals downward.

Consistent with principles of Chinese garden design, nature and architecture are integrated in this scheme for the Shanghai Natural History Museum. As in traditional design, the building approaches the spirit of nature, but does not imitate it. Through its relationship to the site, it represents the harmony of man and nature; its form is an abstraction of two basic elements of Chinese art and design, mountain and water.

The landscape and public plazas of the new museum are designed to integrate with the adjacent sculpture park, while also providing a unique experience for the visitor of the museum, to reinforce its message and mission.

View from northeast

View from southeast

View from west

View from south

Central courtyard

Lobby

Dinosaur hall

Cross section

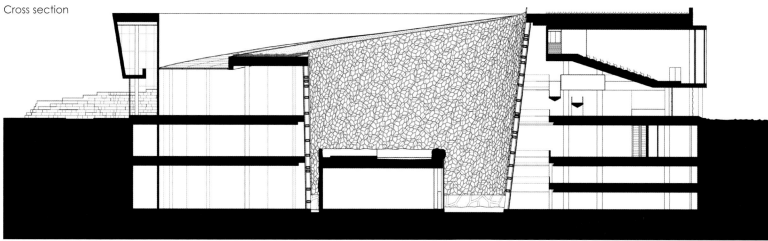

Longitudinal section

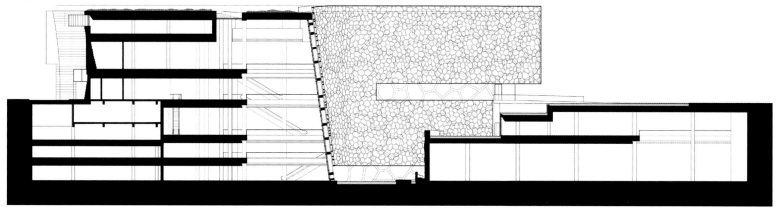

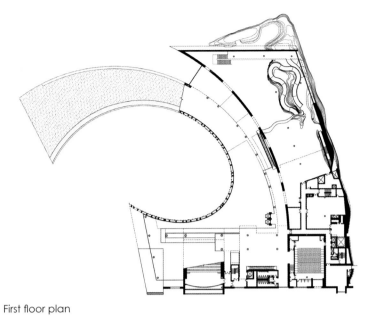

First floor plan

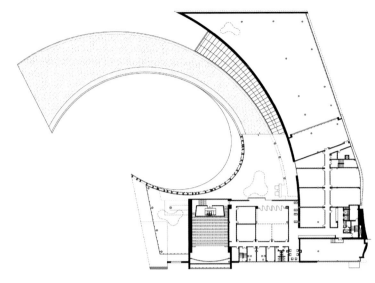

Second floor plan

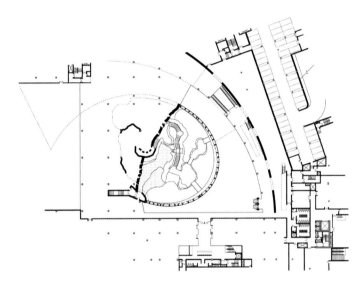

Basement 1

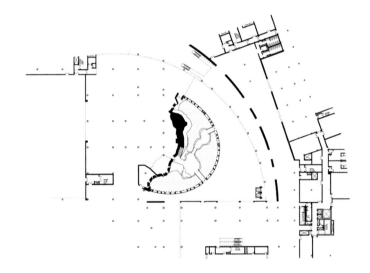

Basement 2

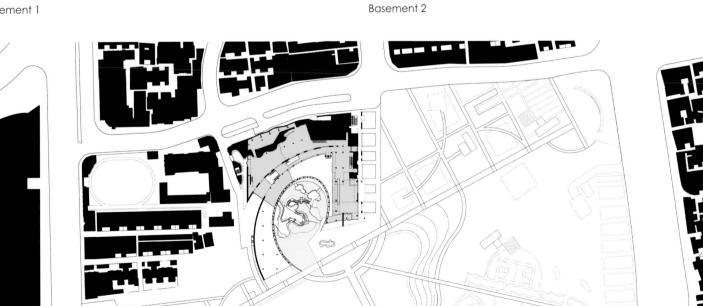

Site plan

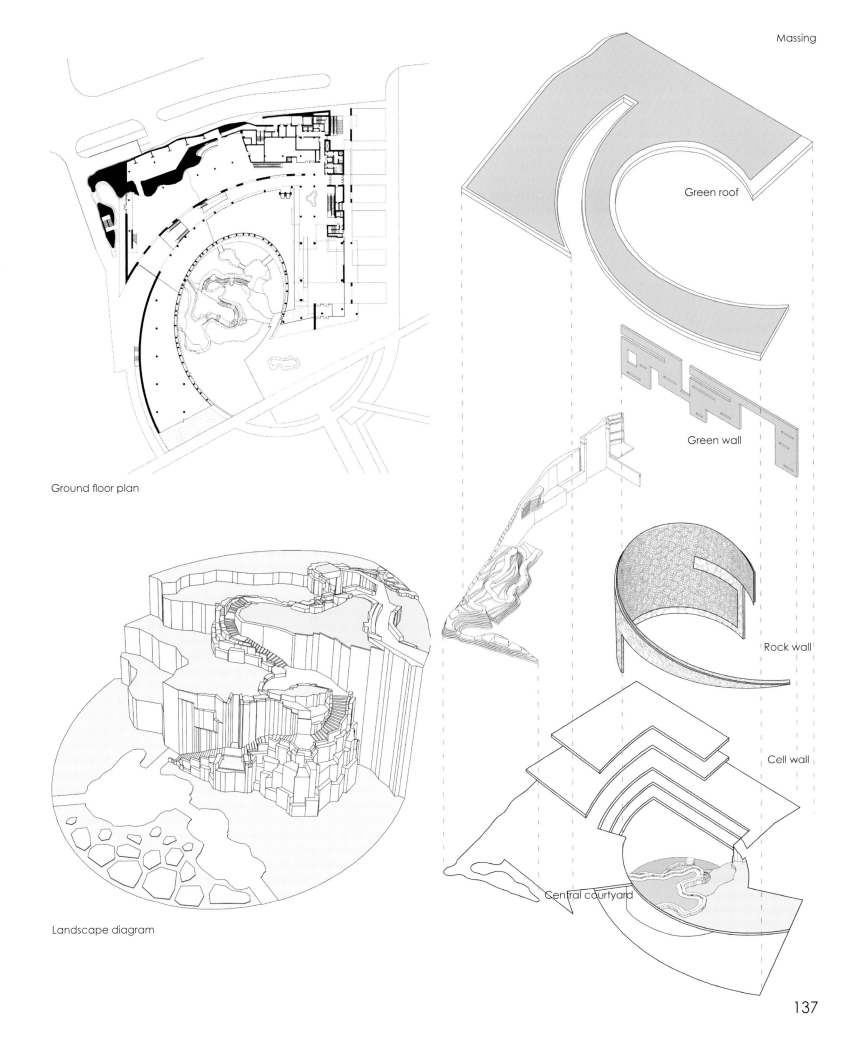

Ground floor plan

Landscape diagram

Green roof

Green wall

Rock wall

Cell wall

Central courtyard

137

Steinhardt Museum of Natural History

Location: Tel Aviv, Israel **Designer:** Kimmel Eshkolot Architects **Competition Date:** 2009 **Competition Name:** Steinhardt Museum of Natural History Competition **Construction Area:** 7,000 sqm **Place in the Competition:** 1st Prize

The concept of the building presents a challenging opportunity to reveal to the public the existence of "natural wonders" currently hidden in the basements of the University. The building serves two different purposes: It contains a public section open to visitors and a section for academic research intended for the permanent staff. The building is designed to separate between these two functions through different areas of activity as well as different patterns of circulation. Yet in designated areas the two functions meet in a series of orchestrated vistas which enrich the experience of the visitor and reveal the work of the scientists.

Inside the building, ramps lead the visitor along the different types of exhibits. Each ramp presents a different experience and is adapted to the architectural essence of the building. In this way, a visitor passes from light to darkness, from open to enclosed spaces, and from small exhibits to diorama-type exhibits. The Collection, which occupies the main part of the building, consists of industrial wooden-panels shell, thermally insulated, so as to afford complete climate control.

Lawn outside the museum

Night view

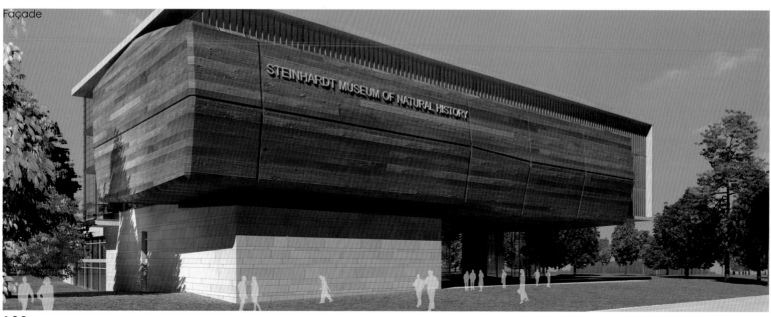

Façade

Stairway

Exhibition space

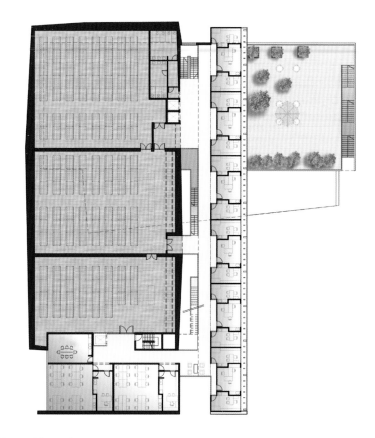

Ground floor plan

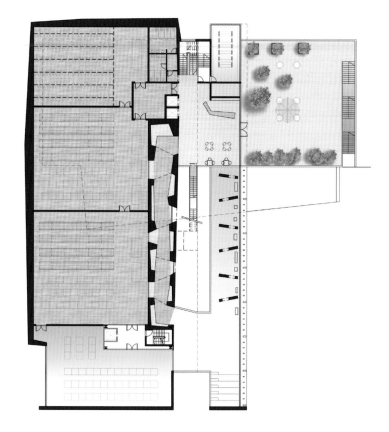

First floor plan

Site plan

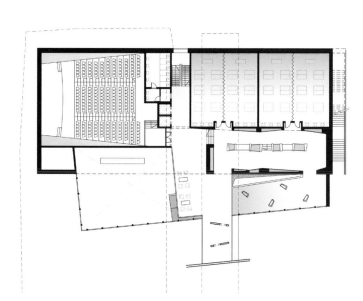

Second floor plan

142

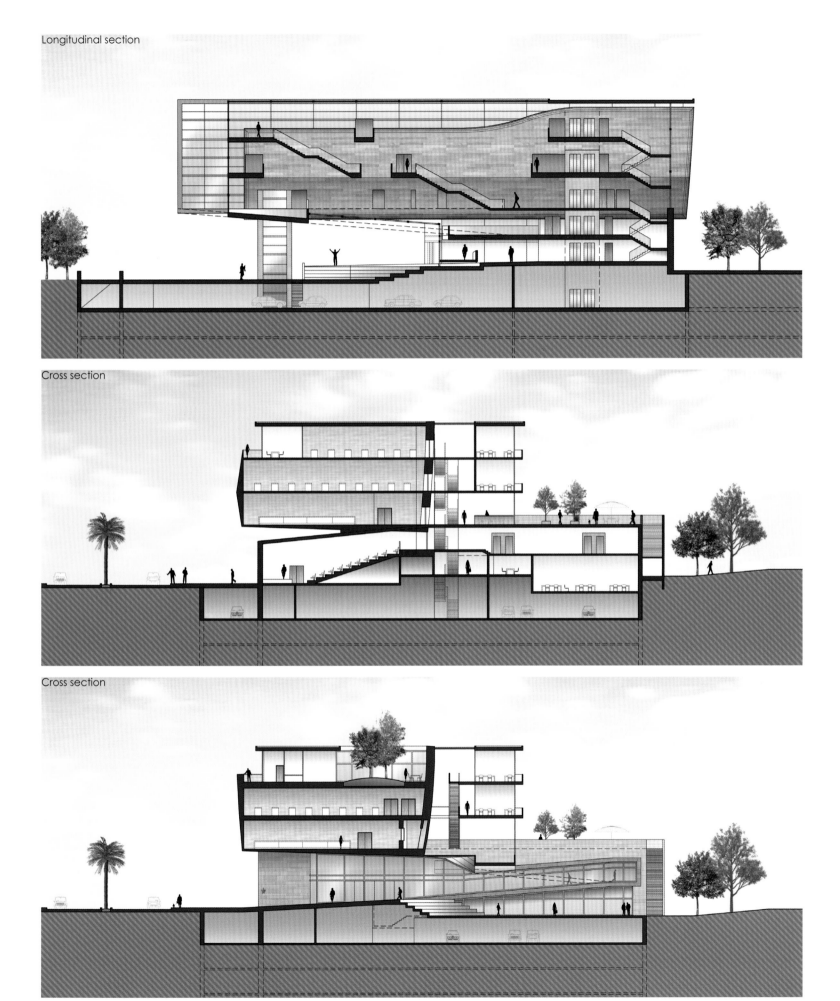

Longitudinal section

Cross section

Cross section

Exploratory Science Museum of Unicamp

Location: São Paulo, Brazil **Designer:** Corsi Hirano Arquitetos **Competition Date:** 2009 **Competition Name:** International Public Competition for an Architectural Project for the Exploratory Science Museum of Unicamp **Construction Area:** 5,370 sqm **Place in the Competition:** 1st Prize

First, the place reveals the indispensable need for the relationship between the new museum and the landscape to give rise to an event of territorial scale. The new museum should become a landmark on the horizon as a geographical fact. A museum that observes and is observed. A building that reveals itself and originates a new relation between Man and Nature, Architecture and Landscape. Second, it is crucial that the new museum should, above all, enhance the value of the institution through its architecture, be the Science in itself. The new building should reveal this aspect, be unique and not just a common structure.

Simultaneously the new building seeks through its design, the primal metaphor between the infinite dimension of the universe and the human property of understanding reality through Science: intervention and landscape, vertical and horizontal, interior and exterior, light and shadow, cosmos and individual.

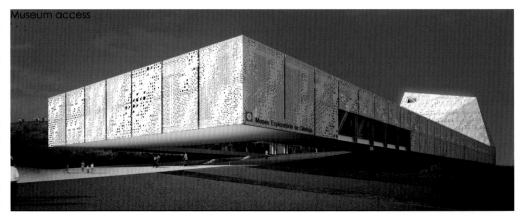
Museum access

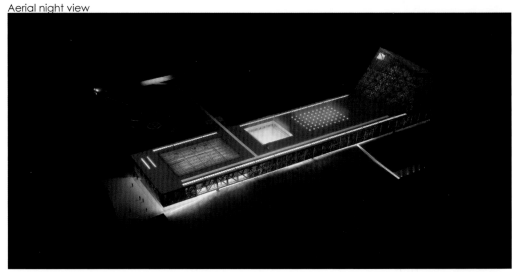
Aerial night view

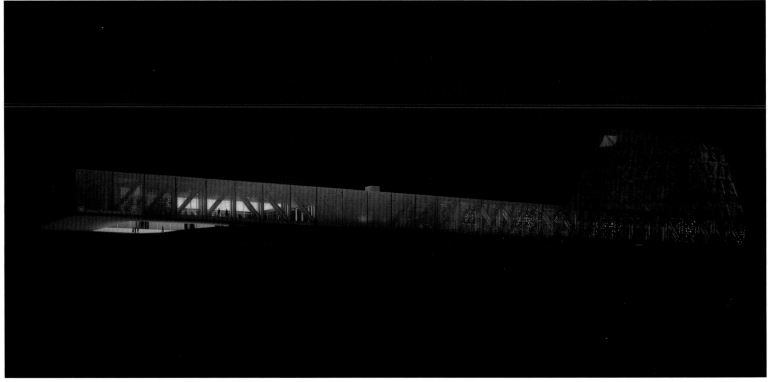

Time space square

Temporary exhibition

Reception area

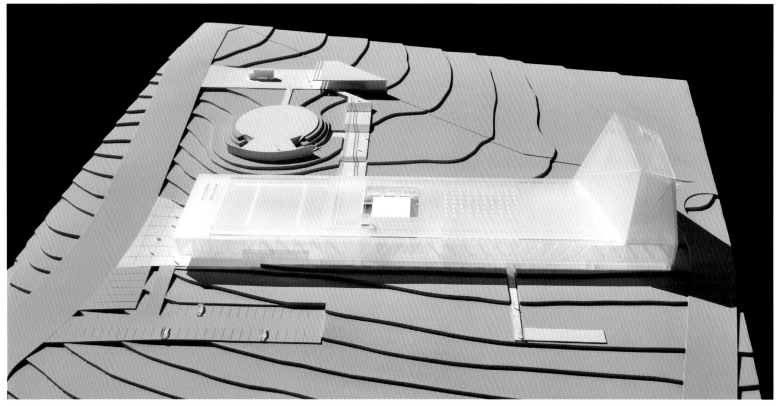

Facade detail

Permanent exhibition

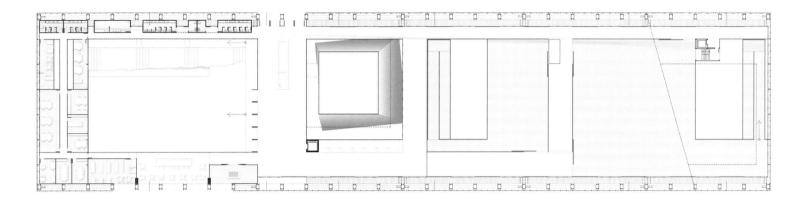

First floor plan

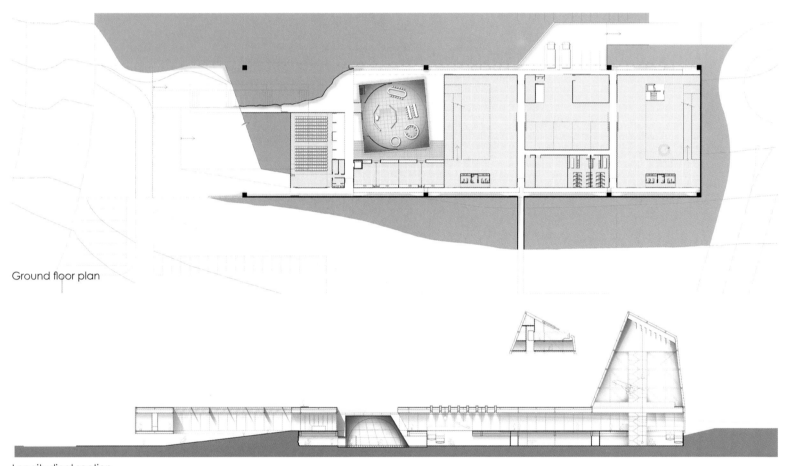

Ground floor plan

Longitudinal section

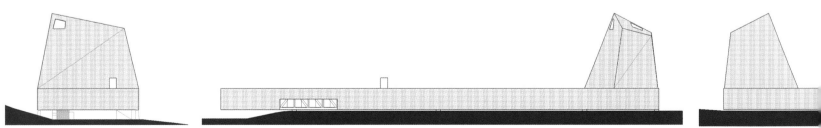

North elevation

West elevation

148

Façade surface concept diagrams

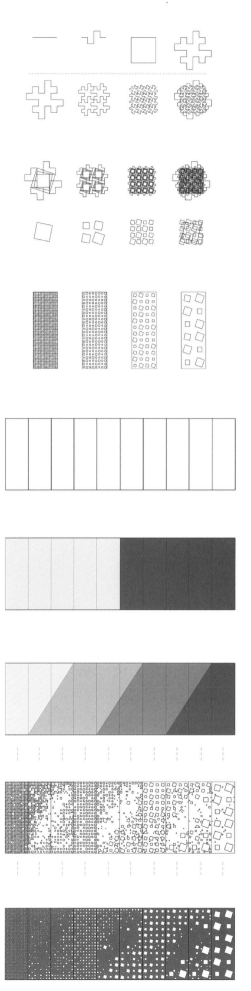

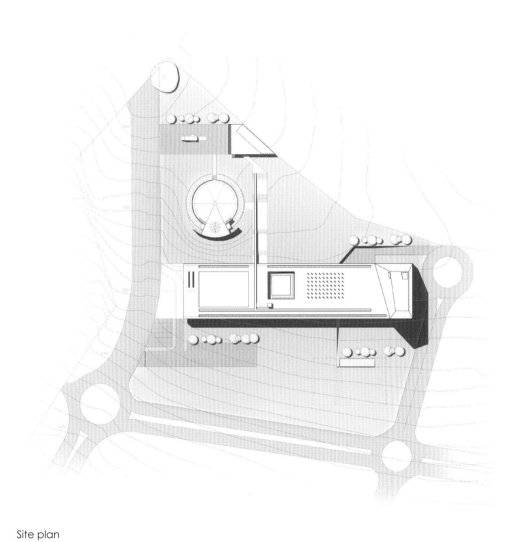

Site plan

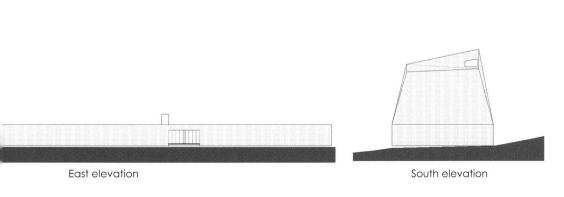

East elevation

South elevation

Danish Natural History Museum

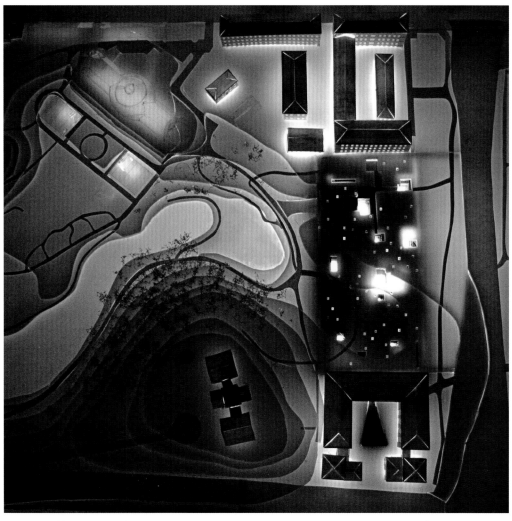

Location: Copenhagen, Denmark **Designer:** Dorell. Ghotmeh.Tane/Architects **Competition Date:** 2009 **Competition Name:** Danish Natural History Museum Competition **Construction Area:** 15,000 sqm

This proposal was founded on an understanding of the rich history. An underground, quarry-like building was designed which physically links the two principal existing museums. Sitting discreetly within the garden, a constellation of glistening skylights recreates the path of the historic moat across the green roof of the horizontal façade. The visitor is led through the excavated space below, which is conceived as a series of platforms and sloping floors, varying in depth. Hewn from the earth, it belongs inherently to its materiality and timelessness.

Numerous routes and viewing points encourage the visitor to understand the museum collection as a comprehensive whole rather than the traditional linear arrangement of many natural history museums. This openness, along with the inclusion of courtyard gardens containing living plants and specimens, creates a theatrical layering of past and present, and a contemporary reading of the cabinet of curiosity. Scale and light are used in dramatic effect to create compelling spaces which encourage curiosity and the wonder of discovery to thrive.

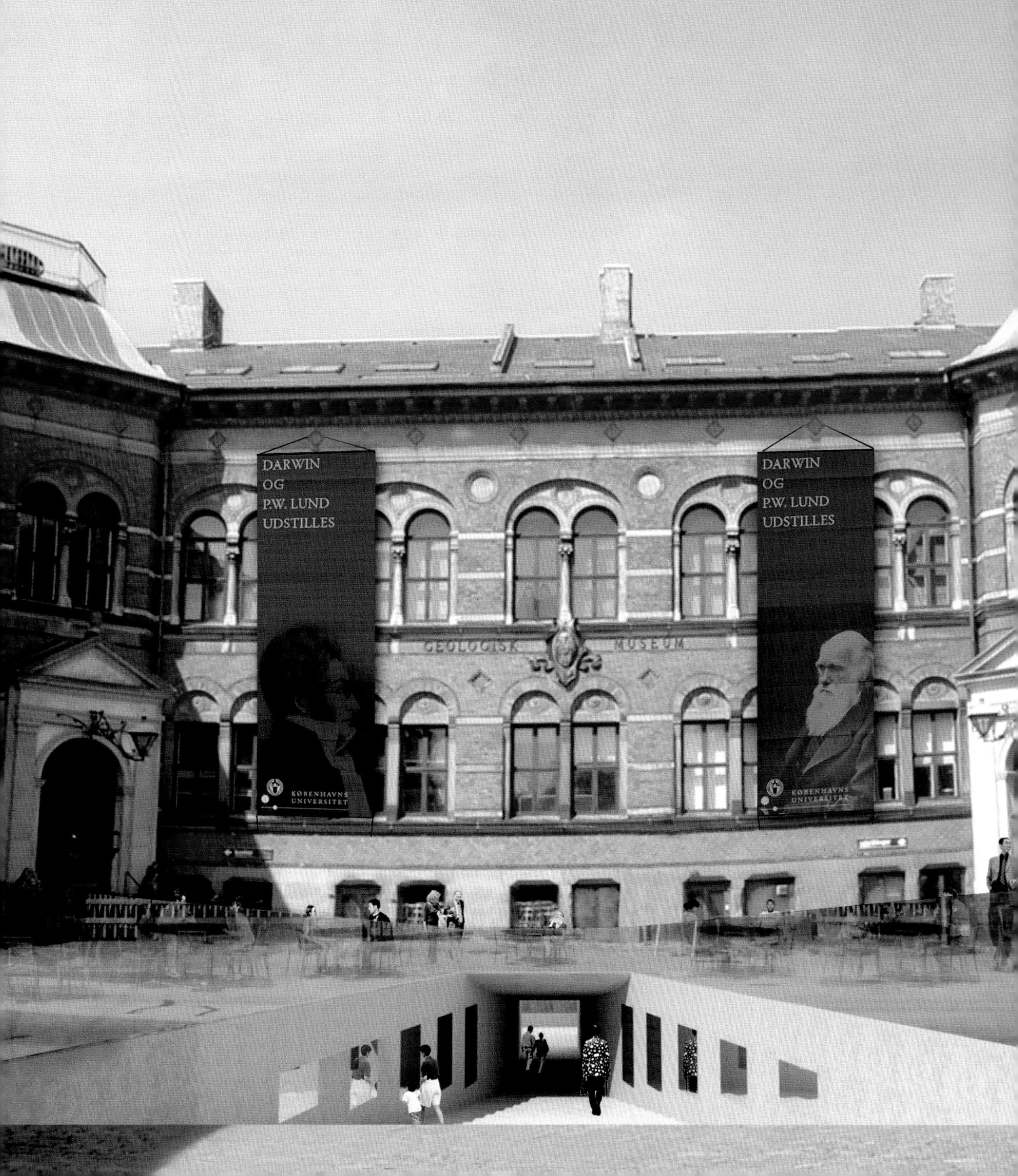

Façade and main entrance

Mineral display area

Tickets

Vegetation display area

Temporary exhibition

Longitudinal section

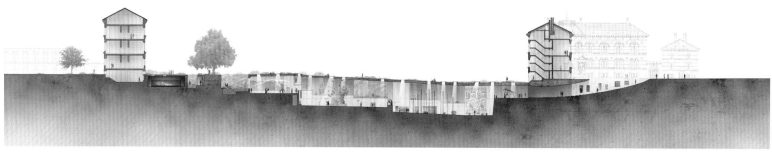

Cross section

Site section

154

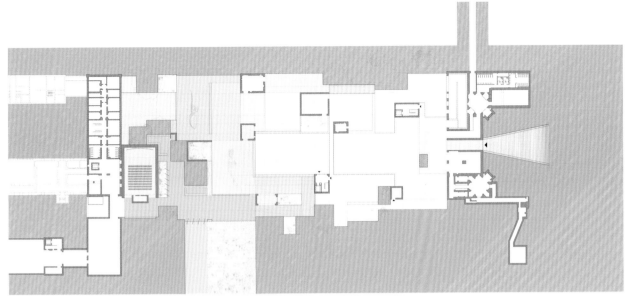

Ground floor plan

Programmatic axo for wall

Extension of an "Eco-museum" in Rennes

Entrance hall from the desk

Location: Rennes, France **Designer:** Guinée*Potin Architects **Competition Date:** 2007 **Construction Area:** 880 sqm

Taking into account a strong natural context, the project shows a wood skin drawing with a graphic pattern, composing a generous scale for a "building-sign", real "Eco-museum" showcase. This formal intention, in addition to its impact, symbolises the programme "Eco-museum", a real exemplary teaching tool, in prospect to a successful environmental integration. Holding account of the will to use natural materials, the designers have chosen the material principle "eco-biological":

The extension of the entrance hall and the temporary exhibition is in timber framework and timber cladding. The use of "dry" producer allows a management of a clean building site, the conservation to the maximum of trees and the continuous use of existing buildings in period of work.

Southern side, the timber framework will put down an ecological concrete wall base and tinted in the mass with natural pigments. Above this wall base, the timber cladding is in natural wood shingles (chestnut) drawing graphic pattern and cover eastern side of existing building with panel-insulating cladding.

Entrance hall

South elevation/entrance

North elevation

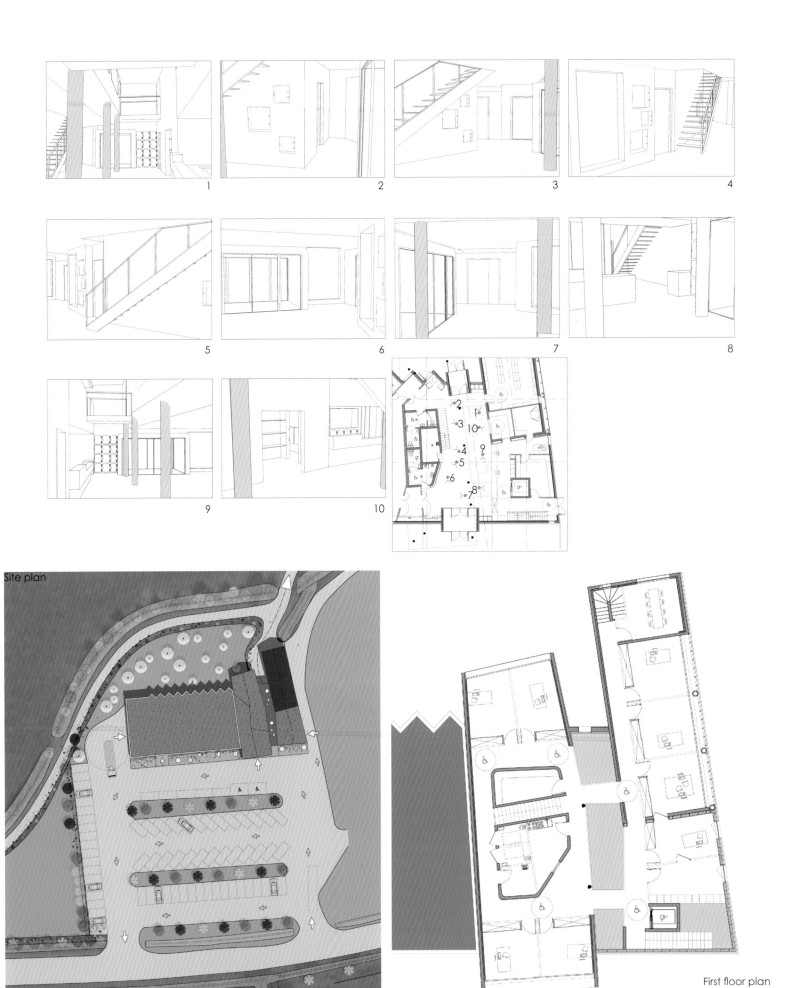

1

2

3

4

5

6

7

8

9

10

Site plan

First floor plan

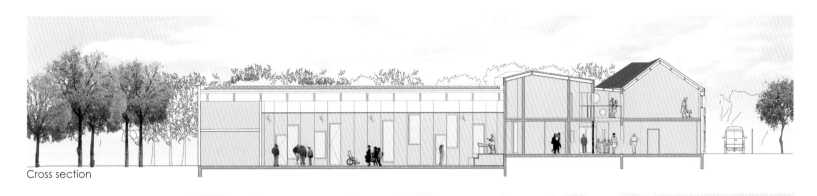
Cross section

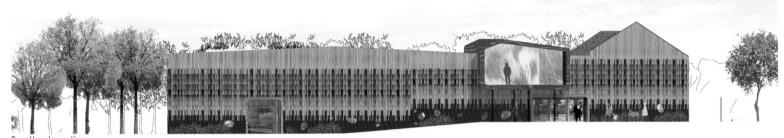
South elevation

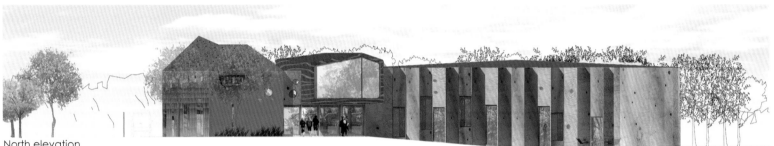
North elevation

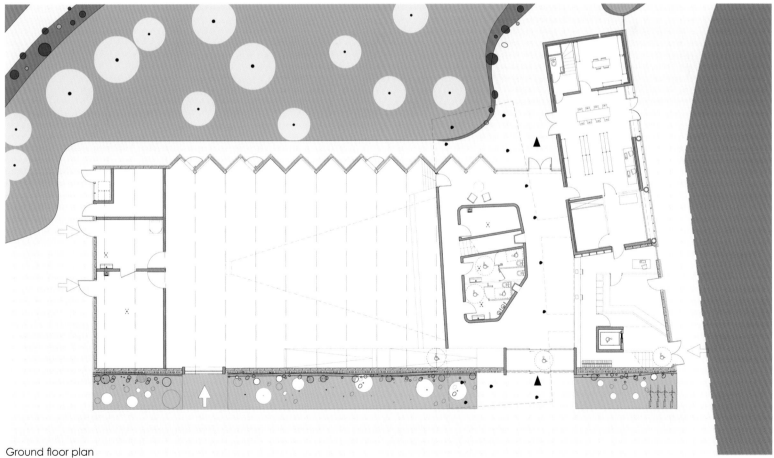
Ground floor plan

Maritime Museum and Historical Centre

Location: Chicago, USA **Designer:** Gerasimos Pavlidis
Competition Date: 2008 **Competition Name:** Maritime
Museum and Historical Centre Competition **Site Area:**
450,000 sqm **Place in the Competition:** Entry

The project is on Chicago's northerly island.
The project's idea was generated by complex
rationales and the historical analysis of the
events that took place in the site. In brief,
the two intersecting axes, i.e. the Burnham's
horizontal axis and the island's vertical axis, are
very powerful. The force of those axes and the
created antithesis bring about a kind of vortex,
like a battle between two elements.
The building is integrated into the park. It is part
of the forces that concentrate at the edges and
deflect due to the physical limit at the end of the
island and the large volume of the McCormick
Place, towards the lagoon. At this edge, the
created disorder lifts the volumes up. The building
grows from the earth and integrates its features
such as the branching of foliage reproduced by
the openings and the land design applied on the
outer surface.

East view

Cable bridge

Night view

Entrance outside

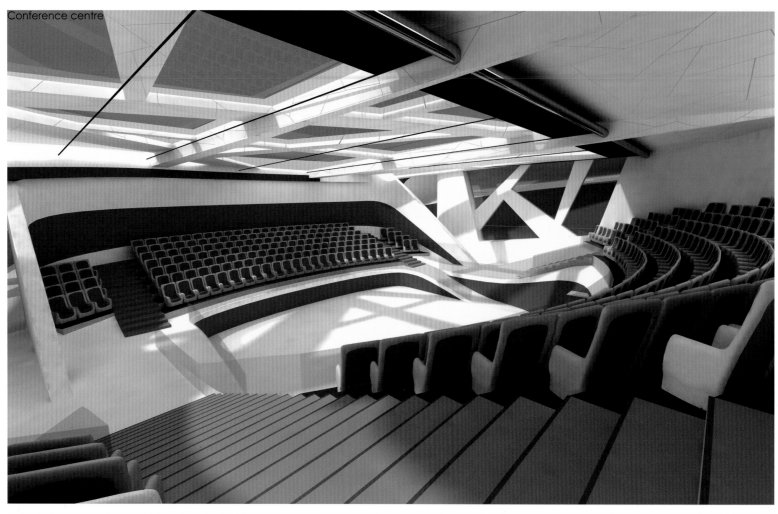
Conference centre

Entrance inside

Structure

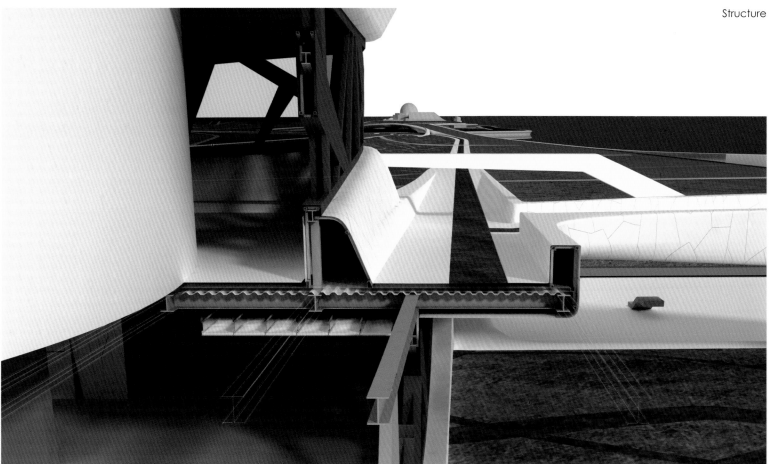

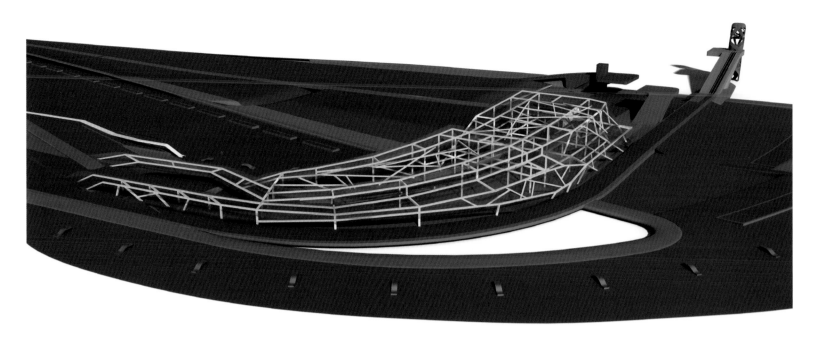

South view

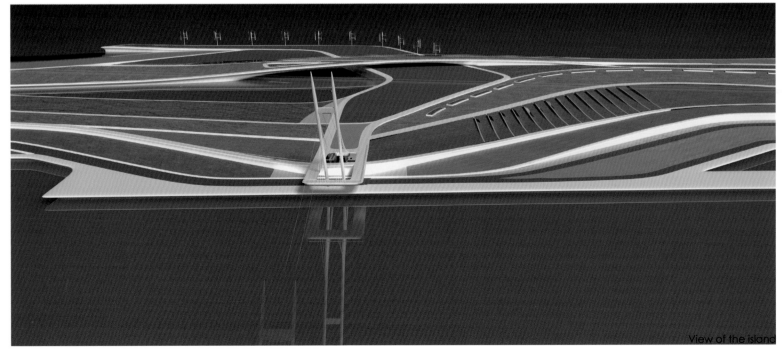

View of the island

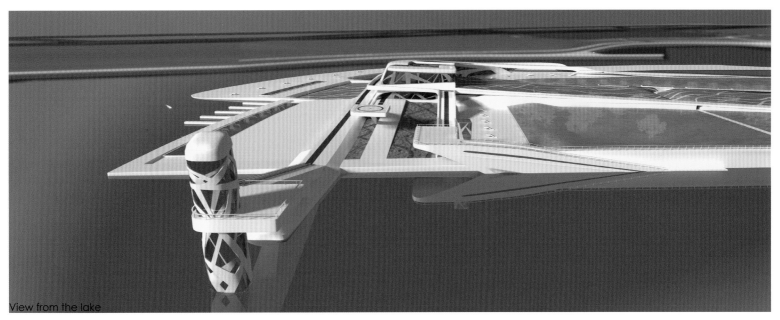

View from the lake

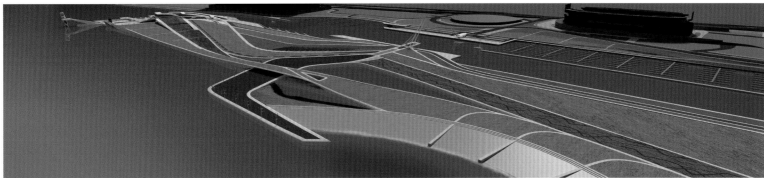

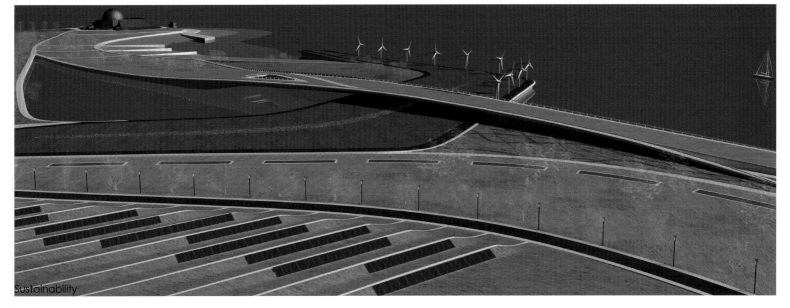

Sustainability

Section

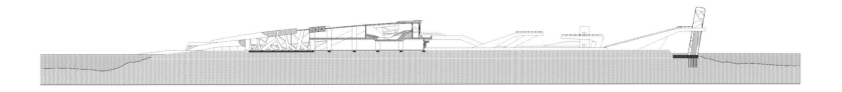

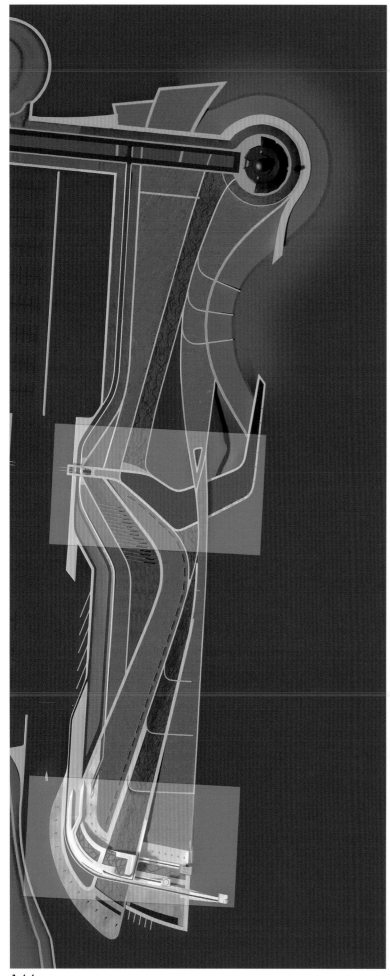

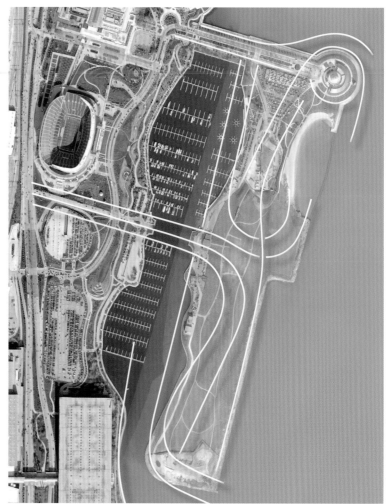

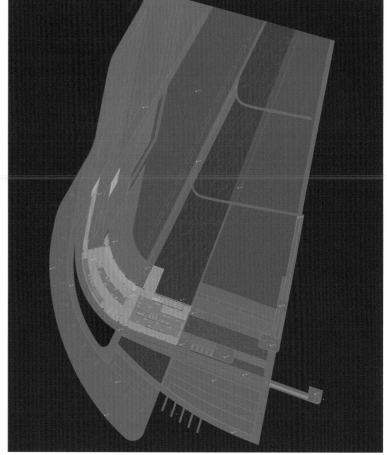

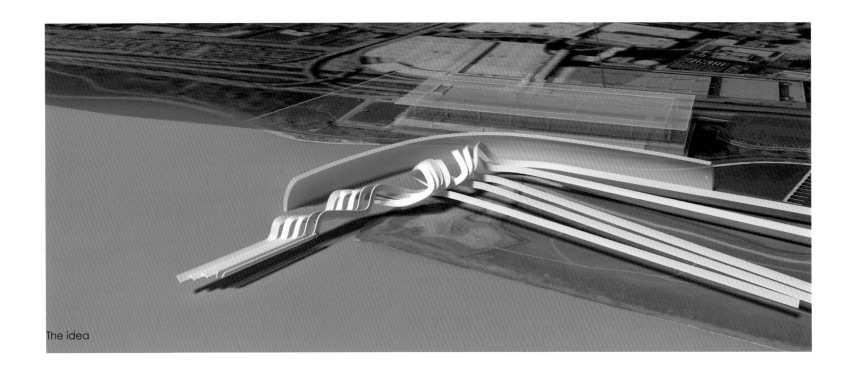

The idea

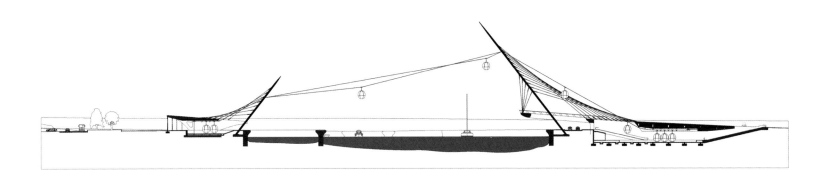

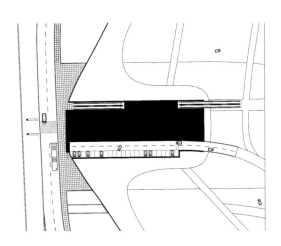

Cable bridge

"Car Experience" – Automobile Museum at Nanjing

Urban exhibitor entrance

Location: Nanjing, China **Designer:** 3Gatti Architecture Studio **Competition Date:** 2008 **Construction Area:** 15,000 sqm **Place in the Competition:** 1st Prize

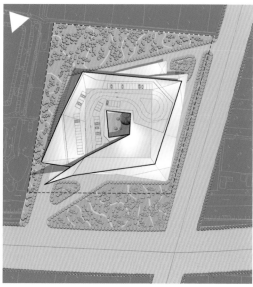

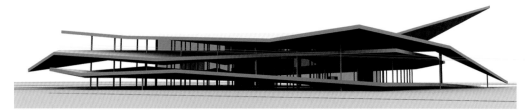

Night view

Here one will not find stairs to different floors, walls or lifts, but ramps which wind sinuously upwards creating a fluid conception of space, and where the flux of cars can move freely and reach the different levels of the edifice.

The principal structure of the building is a spiral ramp with a glass partition dividing the exterior from the interior. In the internal part, reserved for pedestrians, the incline is more gradual, whereas the exterior and steeper side is for the transit of cars.

The visitor enters the museum with his own car and initiates the exhibition's journey as on a safari, going up the external spiral and experiencing a rather "extreme" sensation – as the ramp consists of rapid ascents and descents which create an undulating, uneven surface facilitating the exhibition of cars from different angles and enabling the visitor to observe them from either above or below.

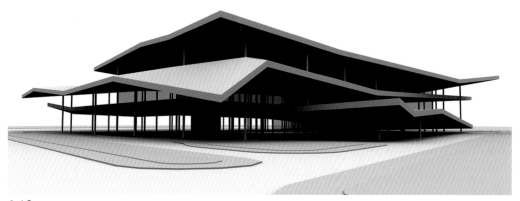

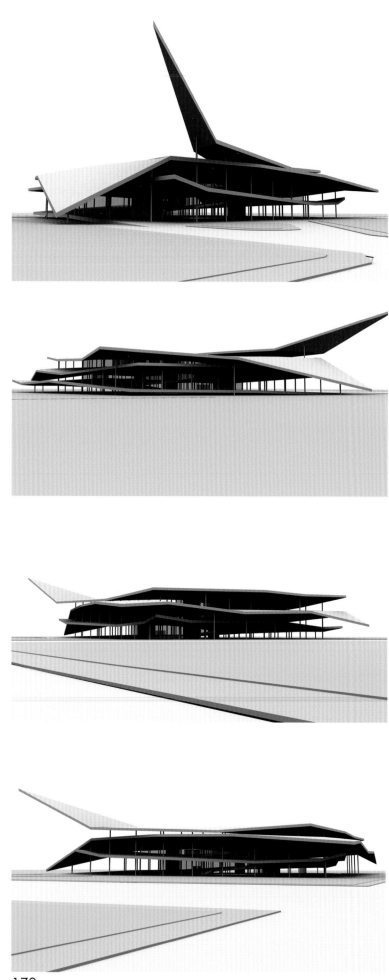

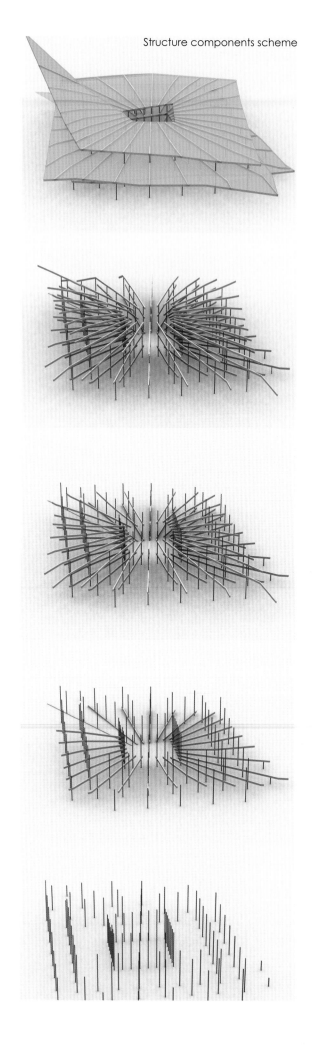

170

Southeast elevation

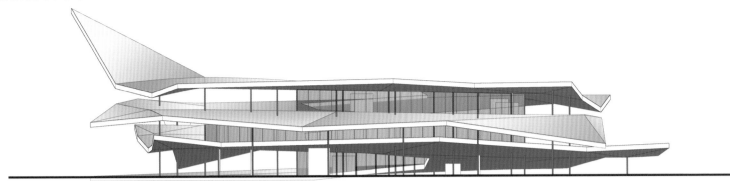

Northwest elevation

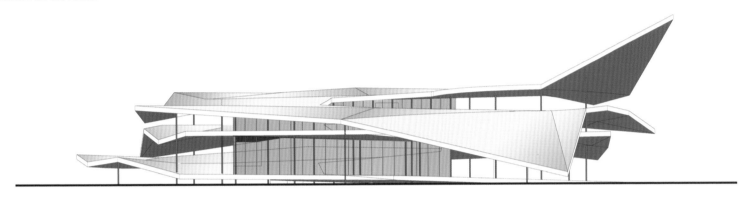

Northeast elevation

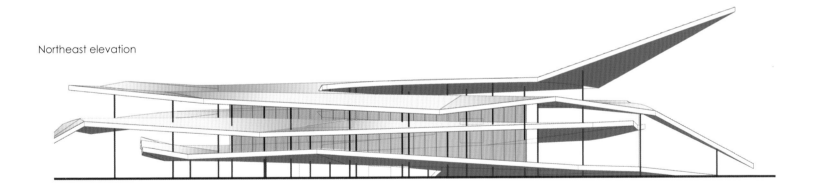

Southwest elevation

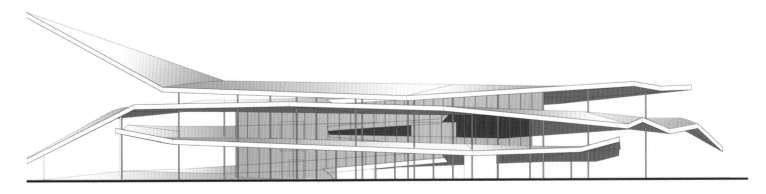

Circulation analysis

People

Car

Air conditioner

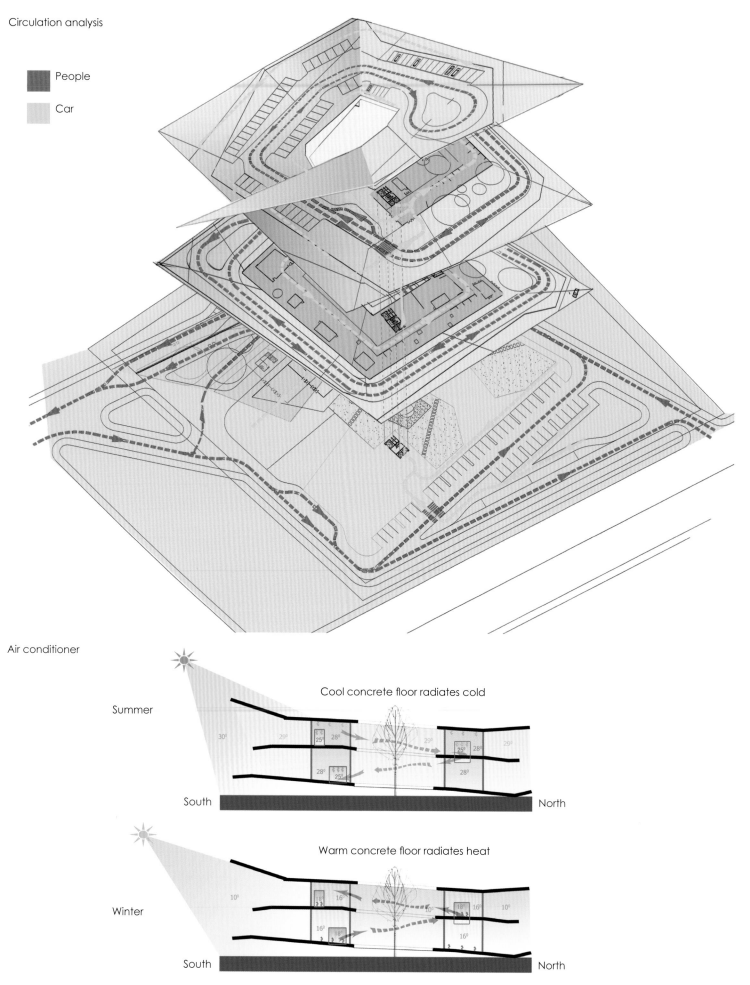

Summer

Cool concrete floor radiates cold

South

North

Winter

Warm concrete floor radiates heat

South

North

172

Sections

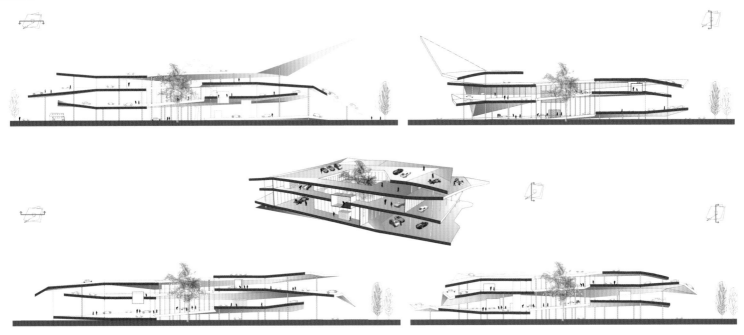

Section

Sunlight

Summer

South

North

Winter

South

North

Ventilation

South

North

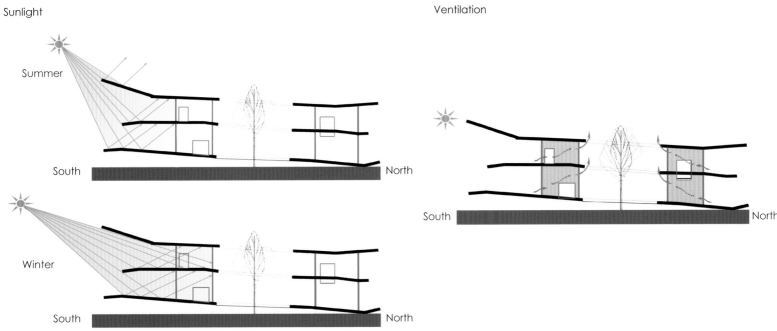

External car ramp

Internal pedestrian ramp

Main glass volume

Glass rooms boxes

Lifts and stairs

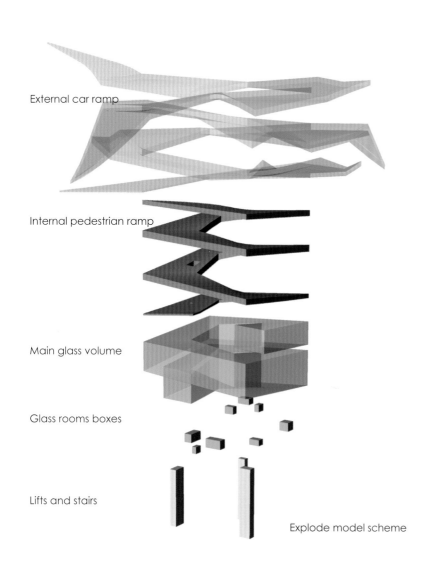

Explode model scheme

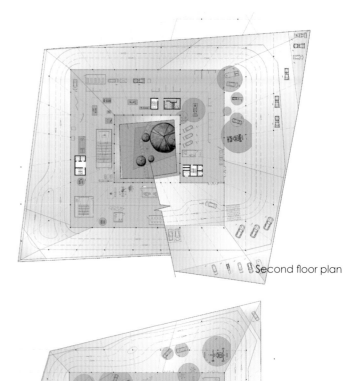

Second floor plan

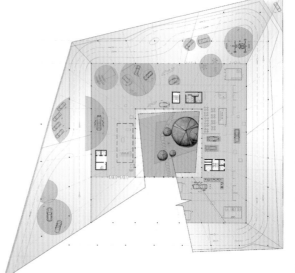

First floor plan

19th century

20th century

21st century

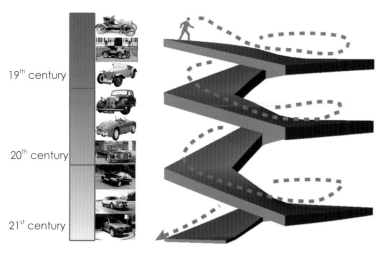

Exhibition sequence

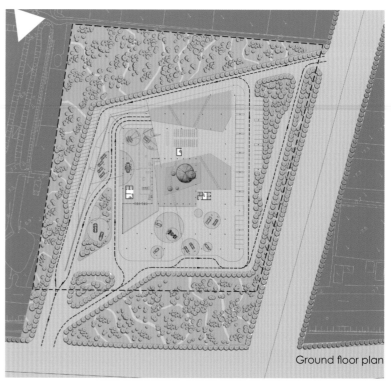

Ground floor plan

View analysis

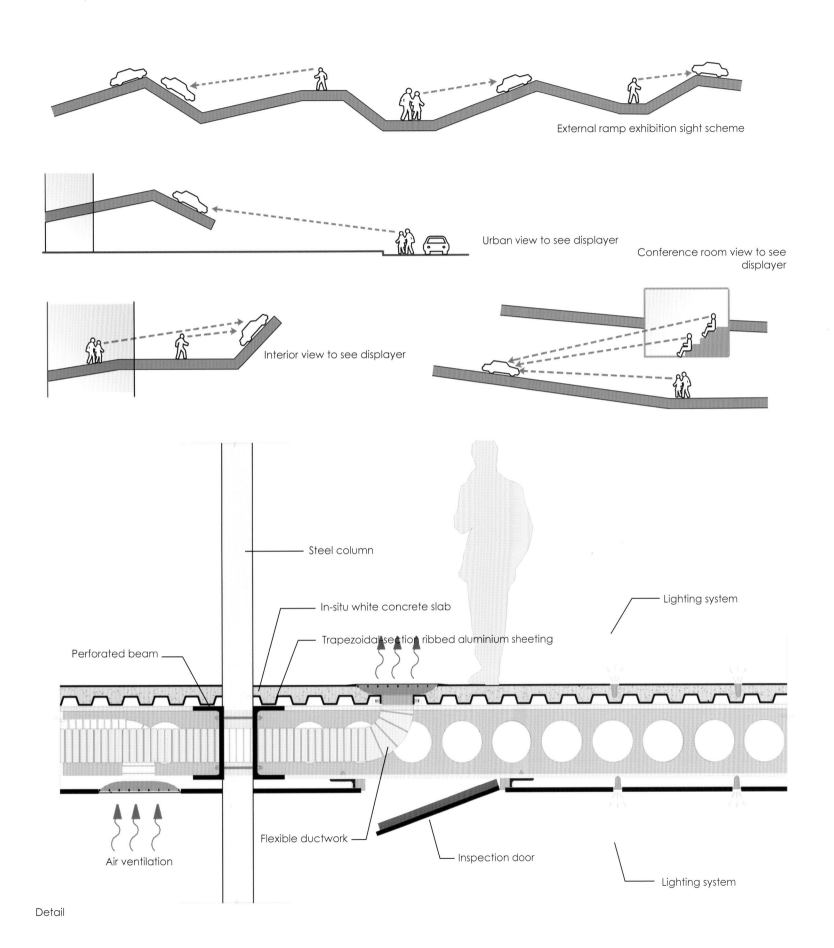

External ramp exhibition sight scheme

Urban view to see displayer

Conference room view to see displayer

Interior view to see displayer

Steel column

In-situ white concrete slab

Trapezoidal section ribbed aluminium sheeting

Lighting system

Perforated beam

Flexible ductwork

Inspection door

Air ventilation

Lighting system

Detail

Shanghai Museum of Glass

Location: Shanghai, China **Designer:** Logon Ltd.
Competition Date: 2010 **Construction Area:** 20,000 sqm

Façade

Situated in Baoshan District in northern Shanghai, the project will be one of the largest glass museums in China. Visitors will not only be able to learn about Chinese and foreign history of glass making; they will have opportunity to participate in the glass making process themselves. Shanghai Museum of Glass will be built in four phases, and once completed it will include: glass museum, educational site, courtyard, commercial plaza and Business Park.

The design consists of an ensemble of both new and old structures; merged together into a functional and iconic design. The new entrance for the museum is placed on a generous entrance plaza, highly visible from the street. The exhibition is located in an old factory hall, which has been designed to strengthen the original character of the existing building. As visitors travel through the museum they will be brought in contact with the series of old and new spaces that create the final design.

On the eastern side of the glass museum a public pedestrian axis leads visitors into the site towards the Hot Glass Show. The Hot Glass Show is an interactive performance most impressive for visitors.

Hot glass show building

Main axis in the park

Corridor

Ground floor plan &1.5 floor plan

First floor plan

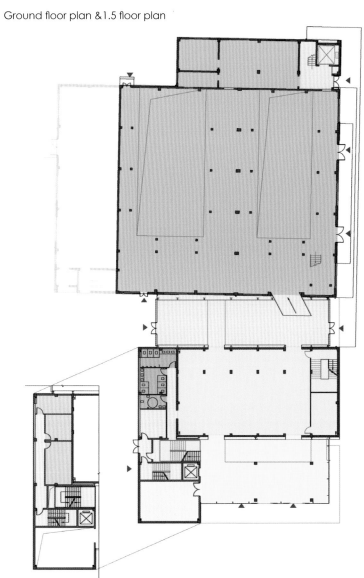

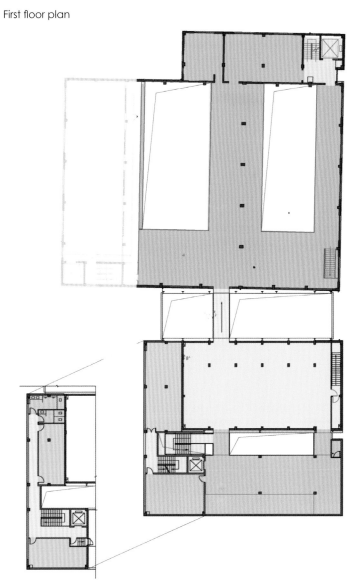

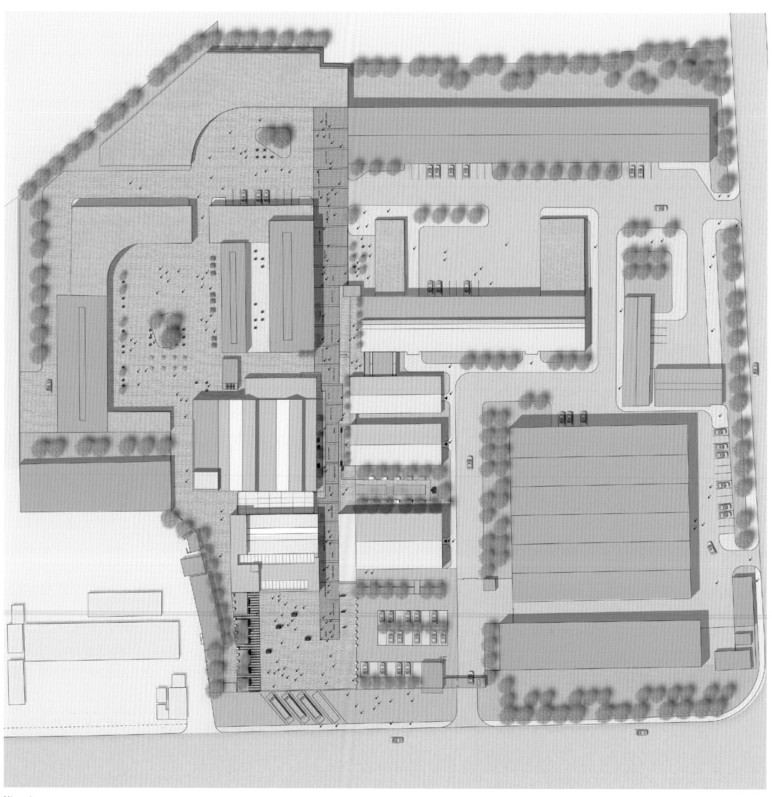

Site plan

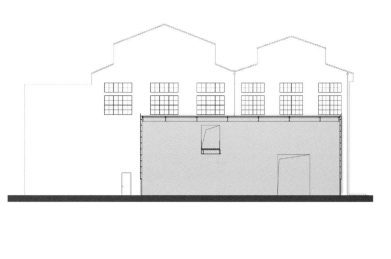

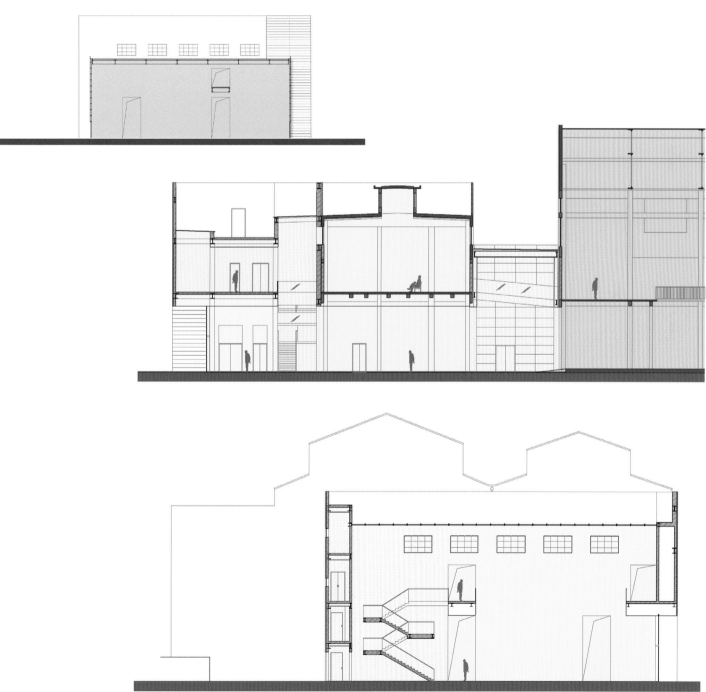

Sixpoints – The Museum of Polish History

Location: Warsaw, Poland **Designer:** Lyn Rice Architects **Photographer:** Lyn Rice Architects **Competition Date:** 2009 **Competition Name:** Architectural Concept for the Future Museum **Site Area:** 29,821 sqm

Sixpoints includes six pavilions which radiate out and define an indoor/outdoor public forum, creating a vibrant, active museum centre – a new hub of cultural and educational activity

and a common point that connects all parts of the museum.

The Six Pavilions are: Entry Park Pavilion with sloped, exterior amphitheatre roof, Rock+Light Permanent Exhibitions Pavilion with monitor skylights, Research/Academic+Administrative Tower Pavilion with indoor/outdoor café and observation deck, Split-Level Permanent Exhibitions Pavilion with adjustable louvred skylight ceiling, Cantilevered Temporary Exhibitions Gallery with landscaped scarp viewing roof, and the Education Pavilion with

its foyer and audience hall open to the park and Outdoor Forum. The Outdoor Forum allows the Park to flow into the museum and creates a sense of place within the Park.

Outdoor Forum and permanent galleries

Indoor/Outdoor Forum and park entry stairs

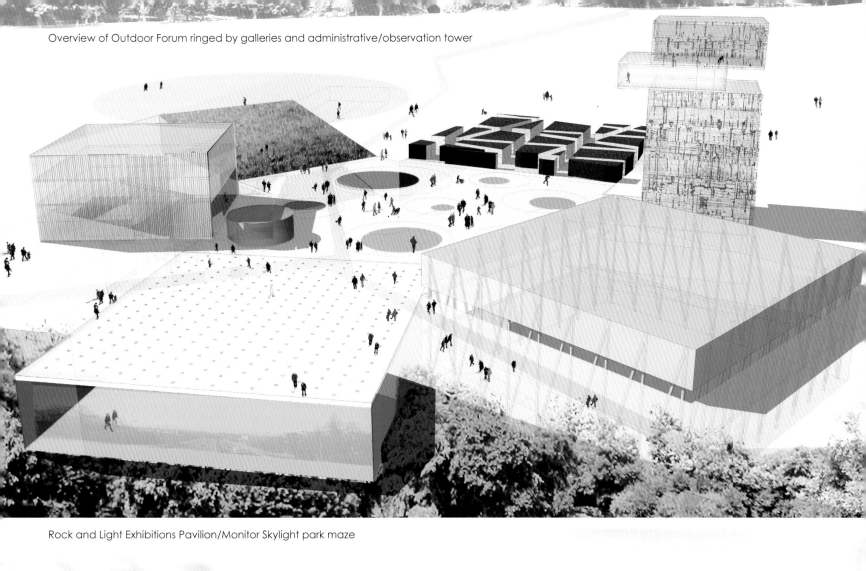

Overview of Outdoor Forum ringed by galleries and administrative/observation tower

Rock and Light Exhibitions Pavilion/Monitor Skylight park maze

Entry Park Pavilion

Indoor Forum with sky-oculi and observation tower

184

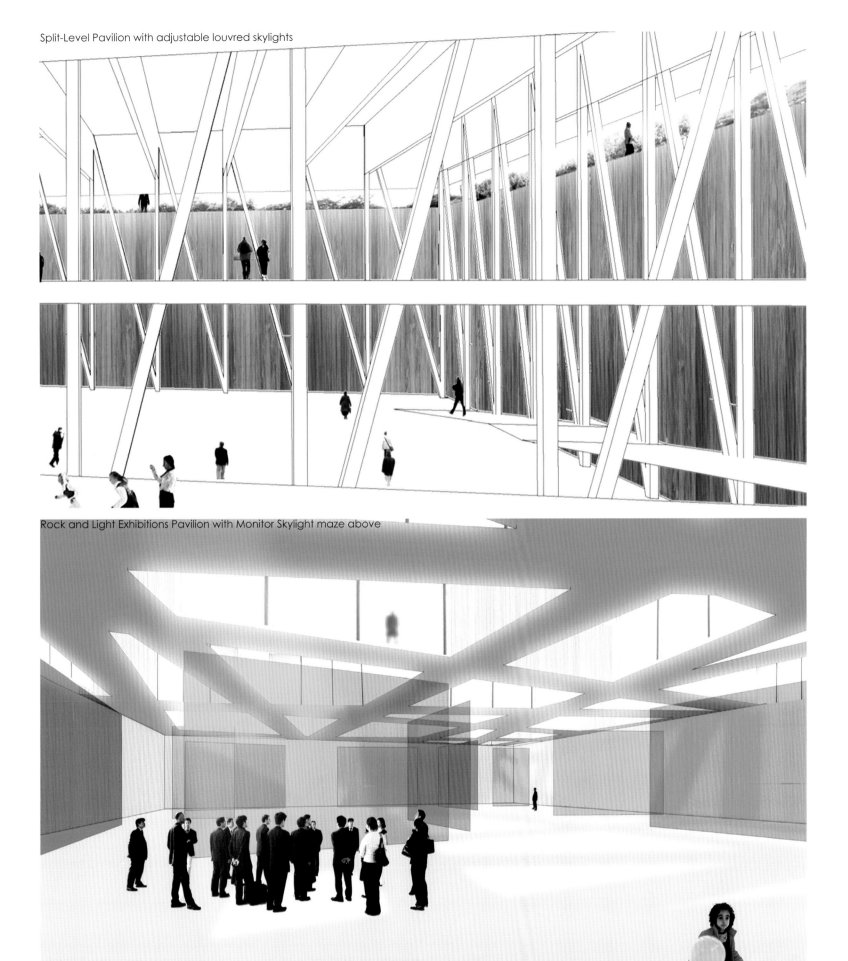

Split-Level Pavilion with adjustable louvred skylights

Rock and Light Exhibitions Pavilion with Monitor Skylight maze above

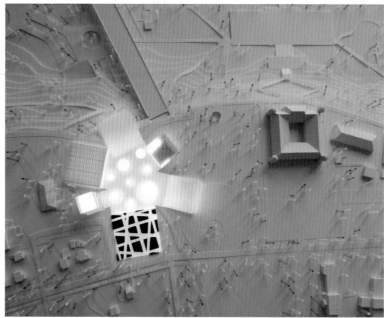
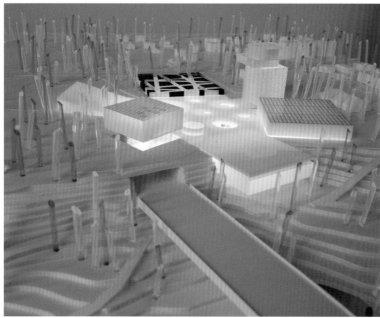

Light cell field at night overlooking scarp

Complementary functions Education & Seminar zone

Public area zone

Exhibition zone

Storage & Garages

Mechanical

Research & Academic
&Administration

Programme

Programme defines public forum

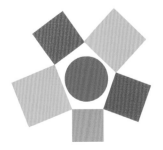

Articulated programmatic
relationships

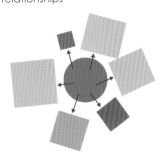

Building remains open to the
landscape

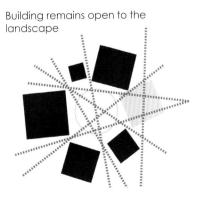

Public/Private

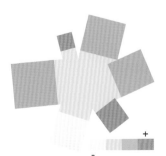

187

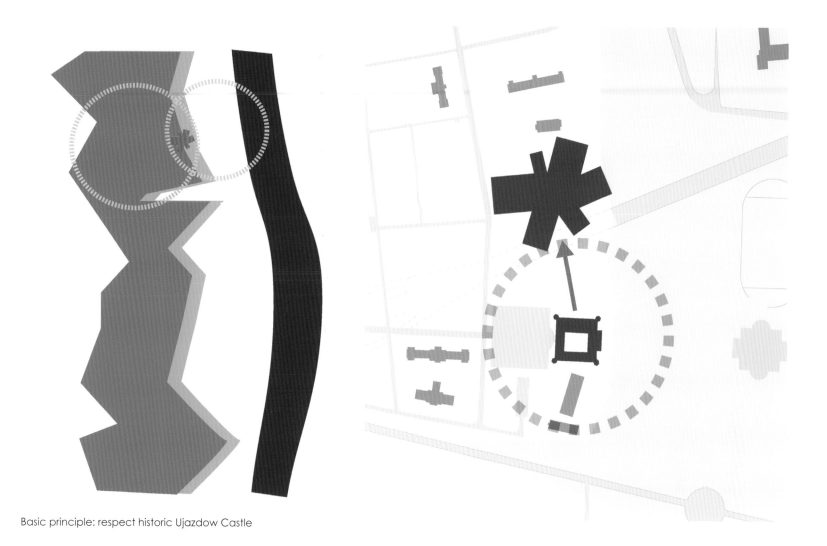

Basic principle: respect historic Ujazdow Castle

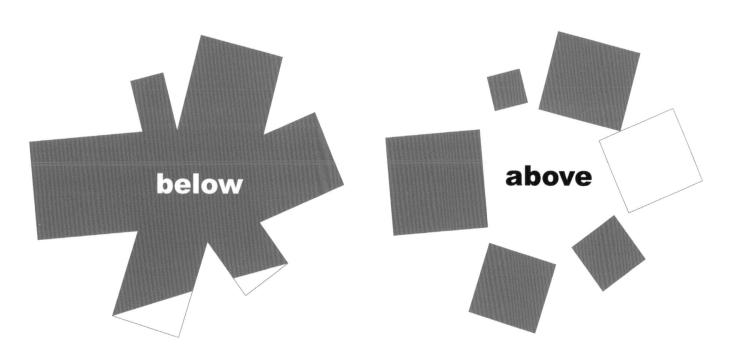

Plan diagrams: above and below grade zones

188

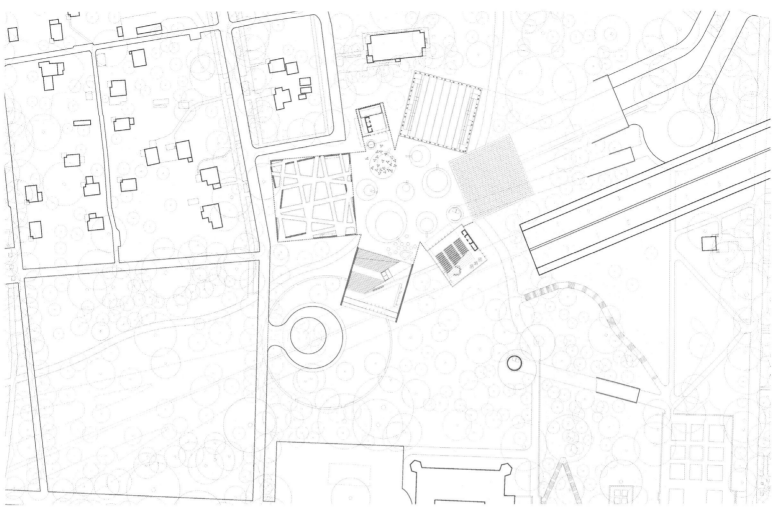

Site plan

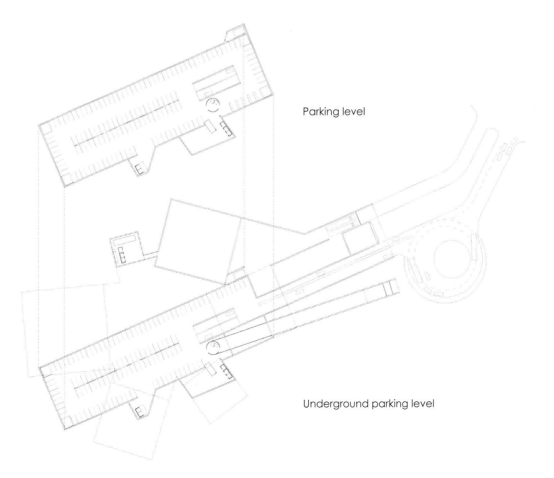

Parking level

Underground parking level

Site plan

189

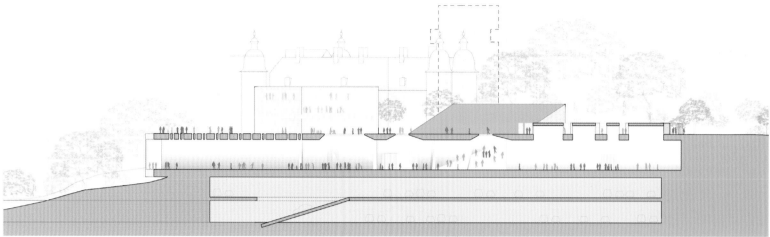

Building section CC through Forum, Temporary Galleries, and scarp

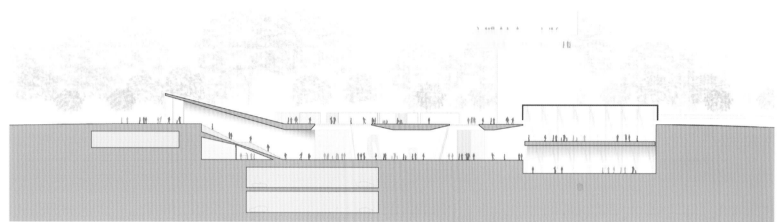

Building section DD through Entry Pavilion, Forum and Permanent Galleries

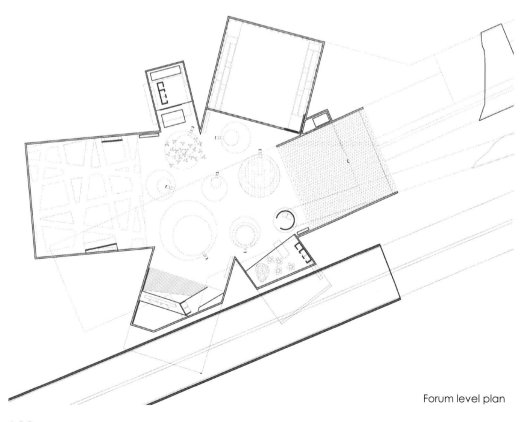

Forum level plan

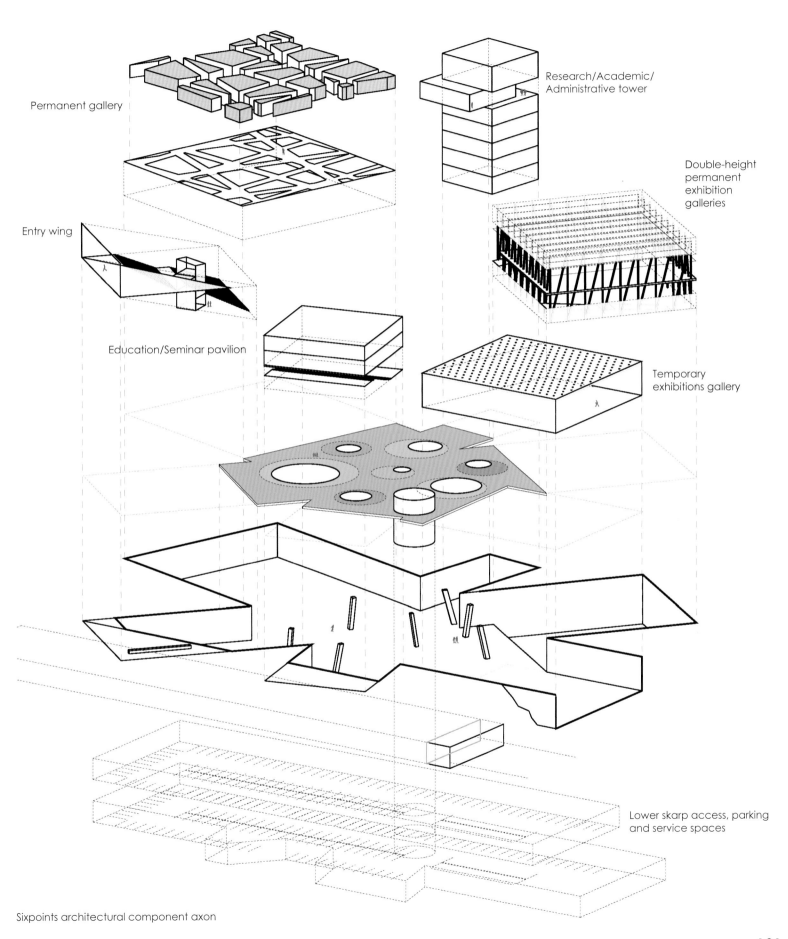

Permanent gallery

Research/Academic/
Administrative tower

Entry wing

Double-height
permanent
exhibition
galleries

Education/Seminar pavilion

Temporary
exhibitions gallery

Lower skarp access, parking
and service spaces

Sixpoints architectural component axon

191

Museum of Polish History

Location: Warsaw, Poland **Designer:** Zerafa Architecture Studio **Photographer:** Zerafa Architecture Studio **Competition Date:** 2009 **Construction Area:** 20,000 sqm **Place in the Competition:** Entry

Awarded reason:

The idea of a "collected memory", one that is inherently fragmented and individual in character in relation to "collective psychology" that represents a group's common ideas and aspirations is the starting point for the design.

For the proposed museum building, the designers have taken a bold step and inverted the typical exhibition space typology. The full exhibit gallery programme is conceived as ten, 3-dimensional monolithic objects, a dramatic departure from the gallery defined exclusively as an interior space. The ten gallery objects are juxtaposed to each other both vertically and horizontally to create a 3-dimensional cubic composition within and through a linear circulation volume. The objects are then pushed-in and pulled-out like drawers to create a series of interior voids and dramatic interstitial spaces.

The ten boxes contain the five chronological divisions for the permanent exhibit programme, the two temporary exhibition spaces, and the exhibition related educational zones. The free composition of the gallery boxes does not determine a particular distribution of the permanent galleries; but provides a flexible environment for multiple interpretations of how the galleries can be allocated and the relationships between them. The temporary exhibition space is located in two of the upper gallery boxes clustered together to provide a multi-height venue for temporary exhibits when required. The "high" temporary gallery is a 12 m tall box which projects out of the eastern façade and through the roof structure to form a dramatic tower-like element suspended within the museum.

East view of the museum

Night view from northeast

View of entry plaza from New Jazdow Park

East elevation

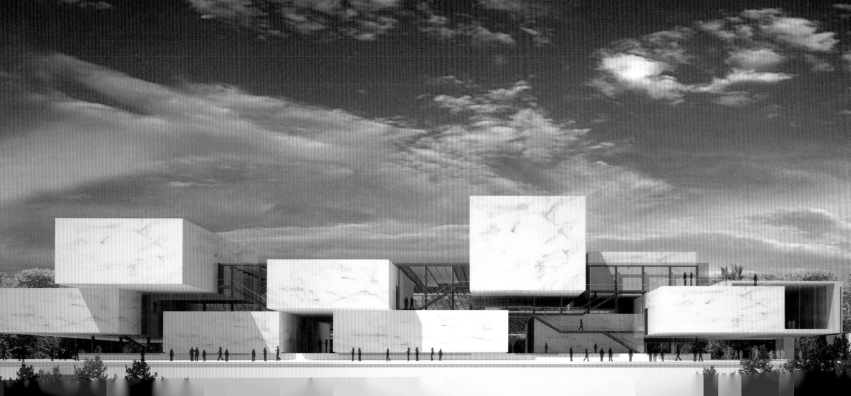

Model photo from southeast

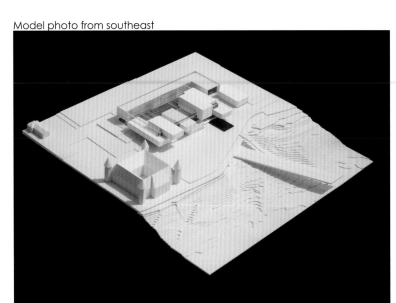

Model photo from northeast

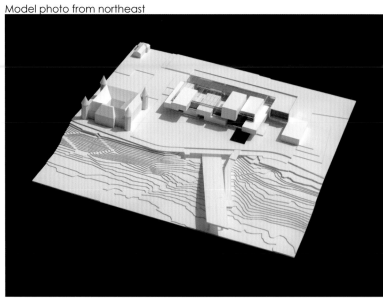

Model photo from east

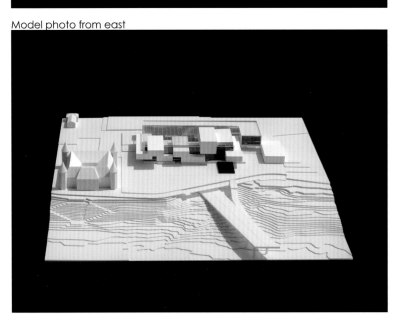

Model photo from southeast

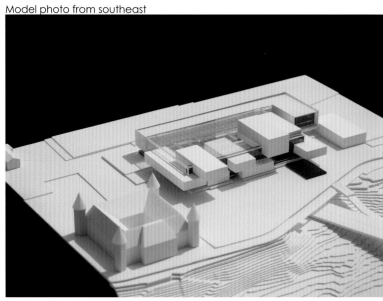

Model photo

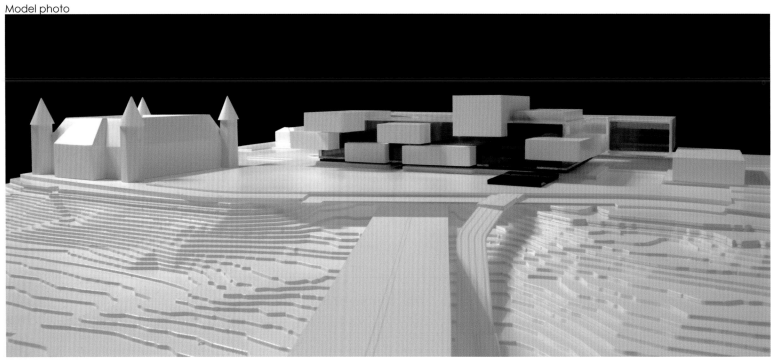

Entry hall

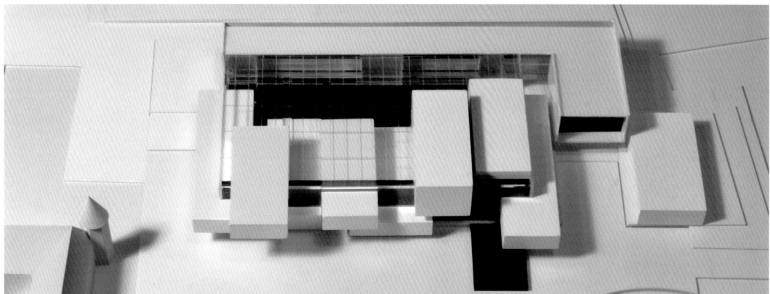

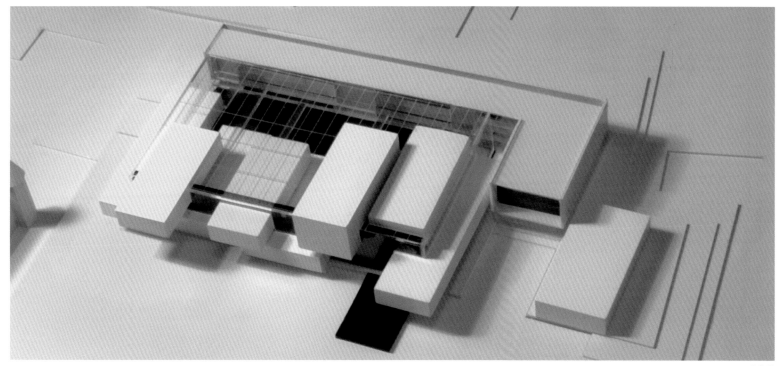

Basement   Ground floor   First floor   Second floor

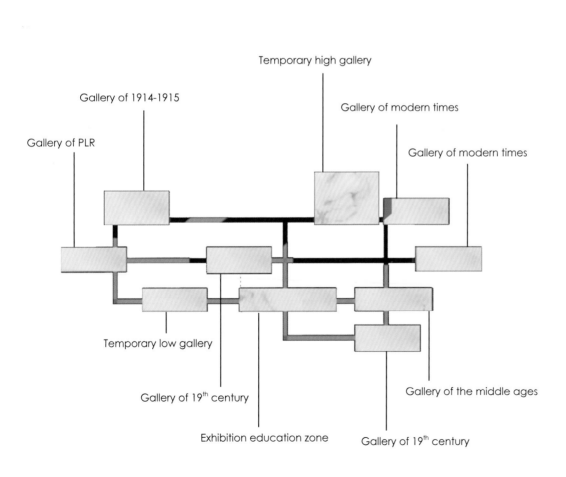

Gallery of PLR

Gallery of 1914-1915

Temporary high gallery

Gallery of modern times

Gallery of modern times

Temporary low gallery

Gallery of 19th century

Exhibition education zone

Gallery of 19th century

Gallery of the middle ages

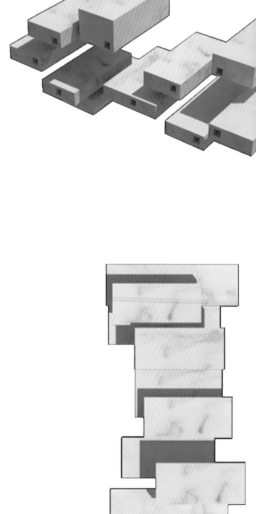

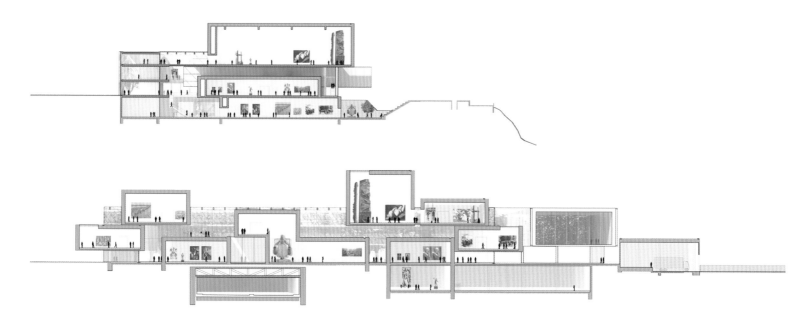

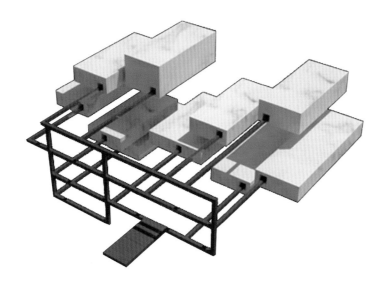

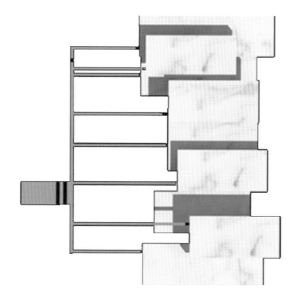

Memory Field – Estonian National Museum

View to the entrance B in winter

View to the entrance B in winter

View to the airfield Memory Field

Location: Tartu, Estonia **Designer:** Dorell.Ghotmeh.Tane/ Architects **Competition Date:** 2006 **Competition Name:** International Competition for Estonian National Museum **Site Area:** 34,000 sqm **Place in the Competition:** 1st Prize

Awarded reason:
The building is observable as a piece of conceptual art, which lends a cosmopolitan flavour to the whole museum.

For this space to be more "vocal", the design proposes an extension of this empty space with a new structure shaped as a long, open hall, a prolongation of the runway axis. The slightly tilted roof – a symbolic reference to a takeoff into the sky, to meet one's destiny – would form a so-called roof plaza overlooking the surrounding landscape. The ascent of the roof plaza sets the stage for a dramatic interpretation of the environment, simultaneously making an allusion to the past events. The designers have opted for a timeless, non-formalistic approach to the architectural design. The building is observable

as a piece of conceptual art, which lends a cosmopolitan flavour to the whole museum. As such, the Estonian National Museum would become a monument to the emancipation, freedom, and independence of the Estonian society.

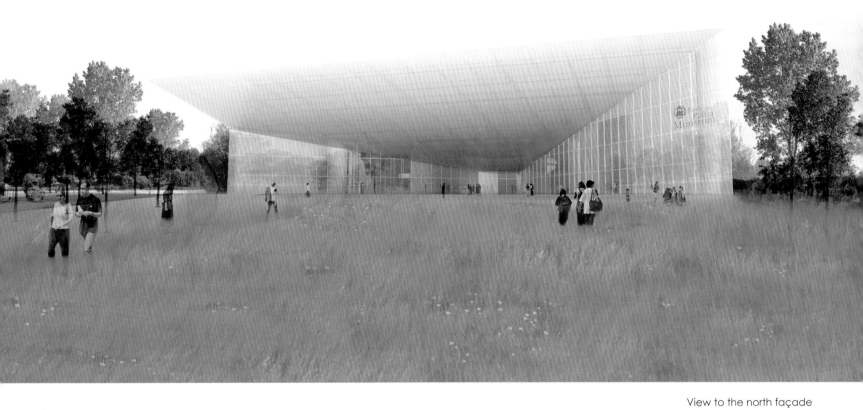

View to the north façade in evening

View to the north façade in winter

View to the airfield with the roof

View to the temporary exhibition

Aerial view

201

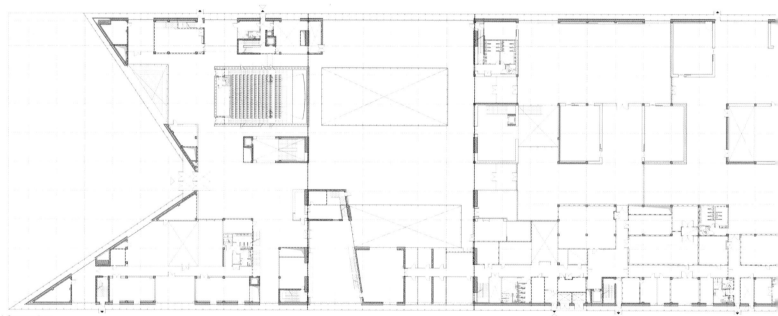

Ground floor plan

Elevation

View to the permanent exhibition

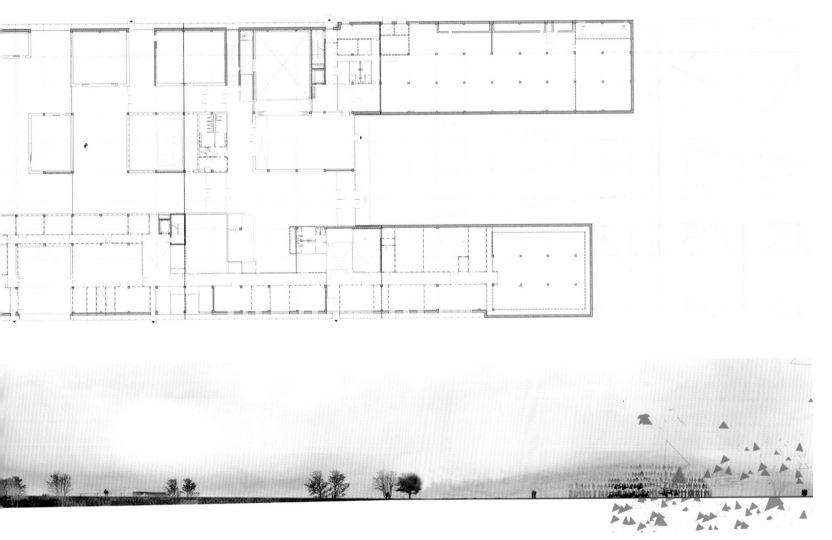

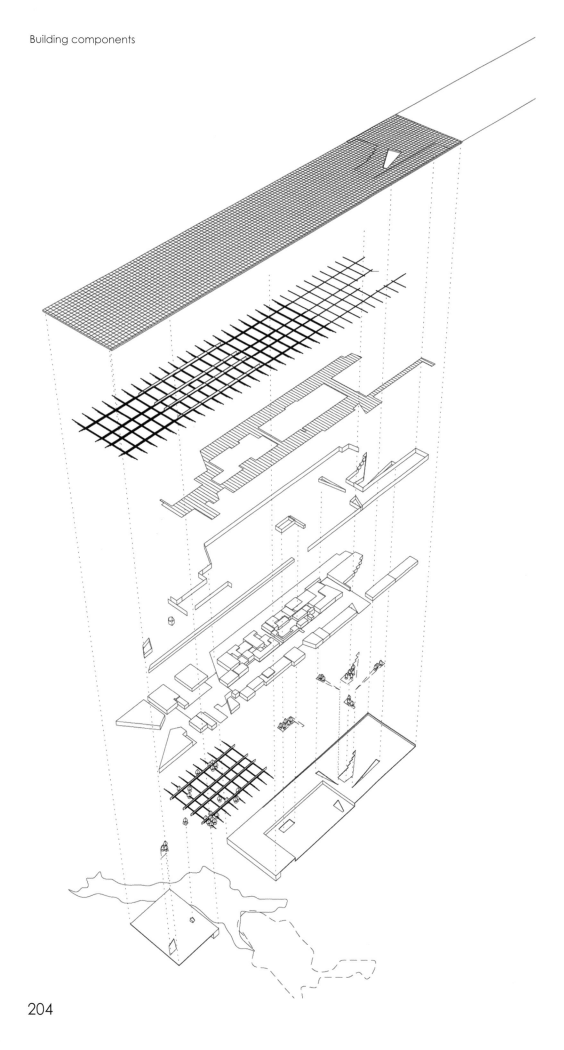

Site plan

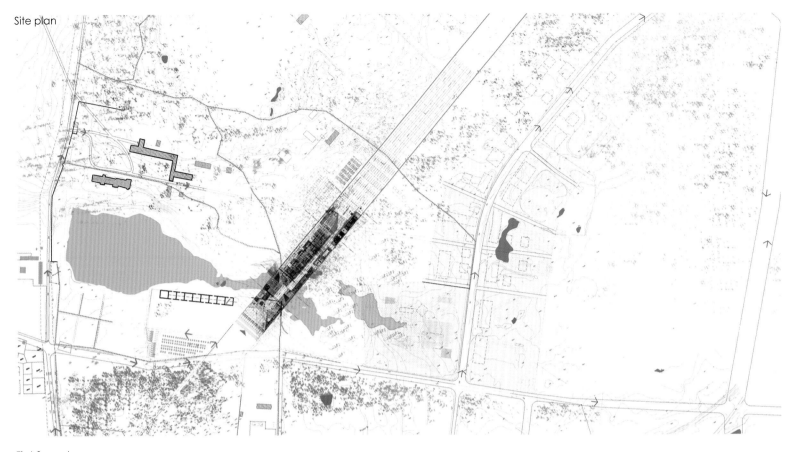

First floor plan

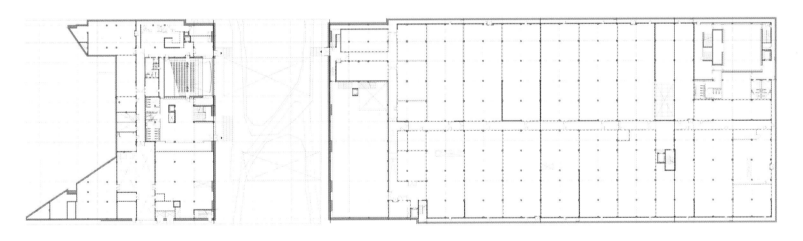

Sections

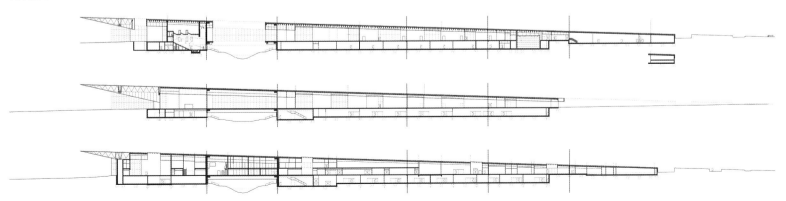

Italian Sports Museum

Location: Rome, Italy **Designer:** 5+1AA **Competition Date:** 2008 **Competition Name:** New Italian Sports Museum Competition **Construction Area:** 15,760 sqm

The project for the Museum of Sport in Rome, designed as a rational division into three of the overall structure, works along the lines of sporting-methodological symbology.

The double-height entrance hall immediately provides a glimpse of a large section of the cone-shaped truncated skylight symbolising Mount Olympus set along the axis with the north entrance: thematic projections will be shown inside and on the outside surface.

The exhibition area, concentrated in the part of the building facing south, is designed like a sort of temple constructed over three levels, with a perimeter colonnade and internal cell hosting thematic exhibitions.

The central section is double height in order to emphasise the main entrance and hall; the part holding strictly exhibition spaces is located on the second and top level of the building and is designed as a multi-storey space supported by exposed columns facing towards the outside through a glazed façade.

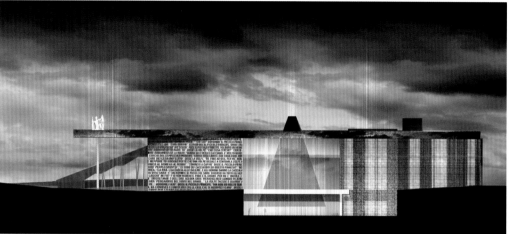

East elevation

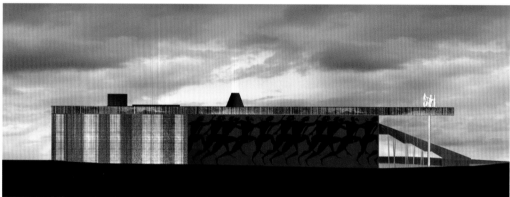

West elevation

North elevation

South elevation

Exhibition space

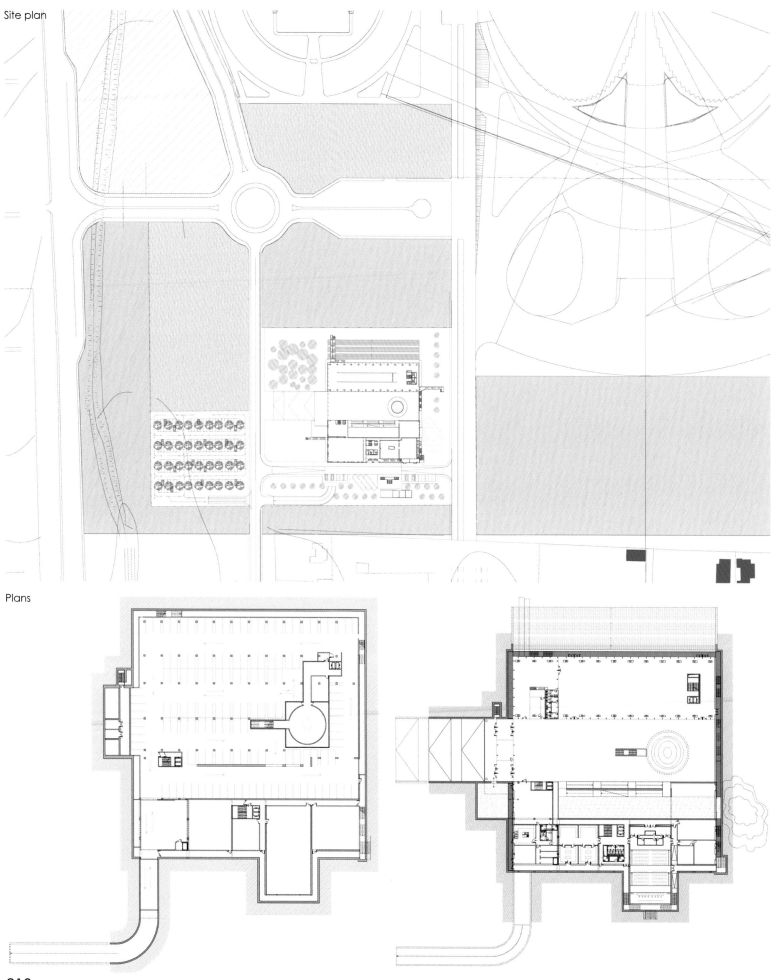

Site plan

Plans

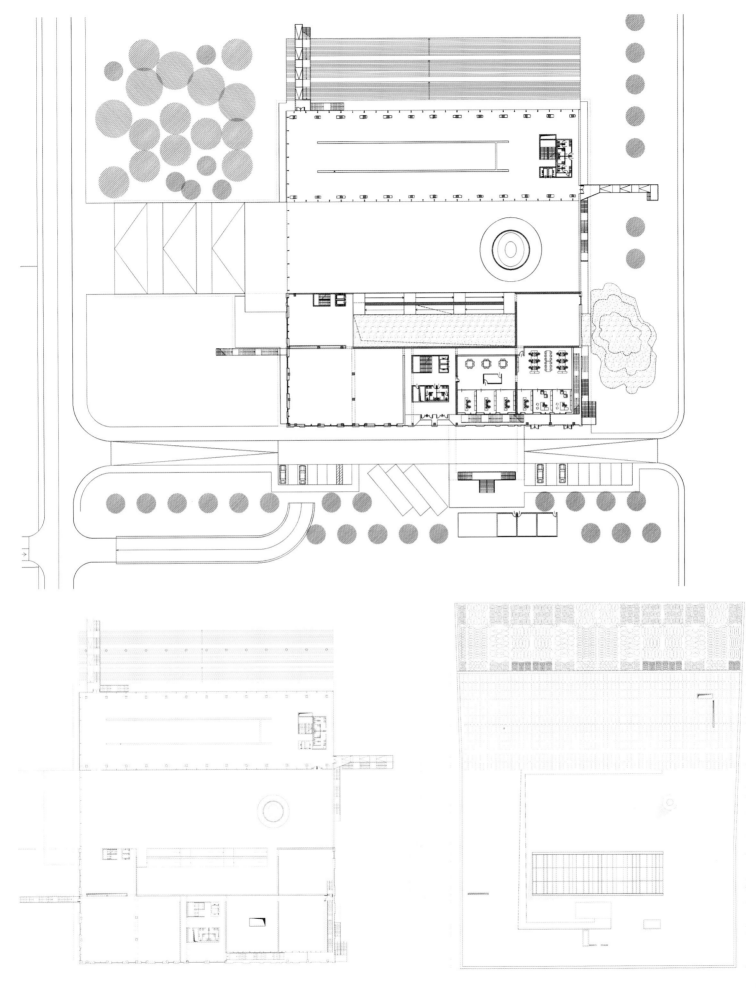

211

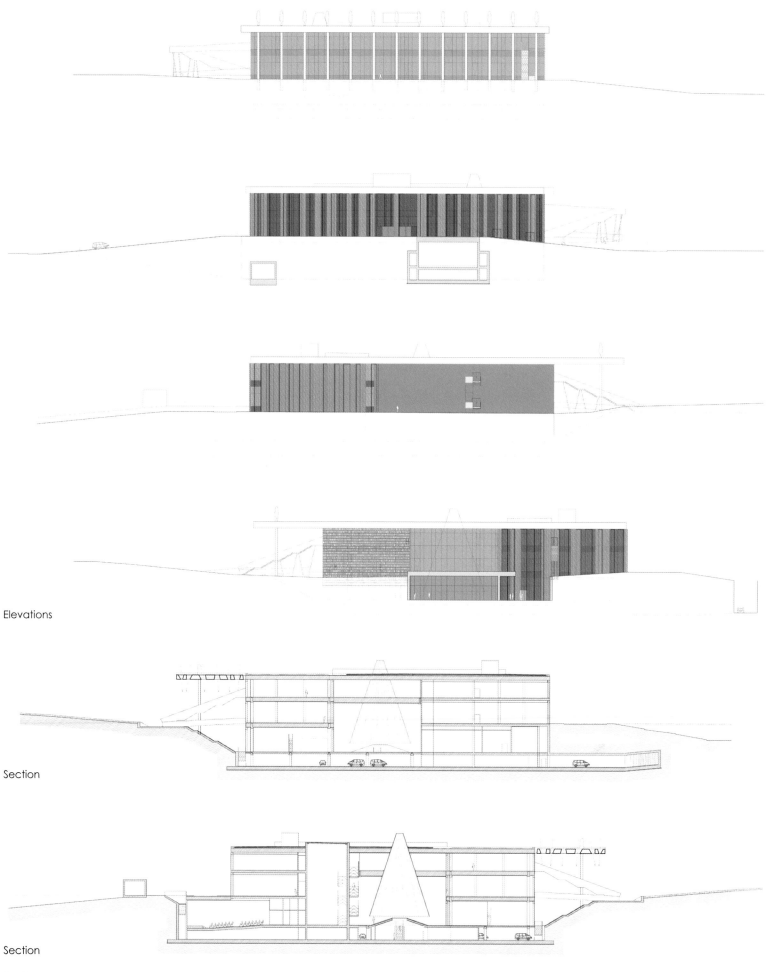

Elevations

Section

Section

212

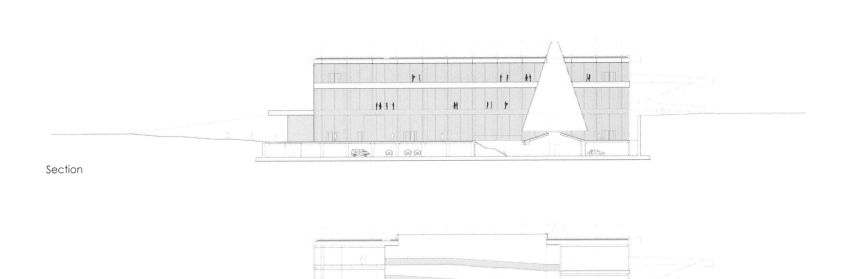

Section

Section

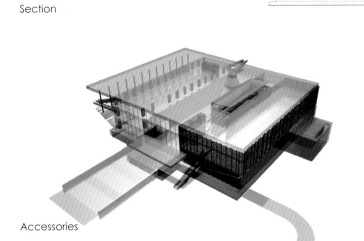

Accessories

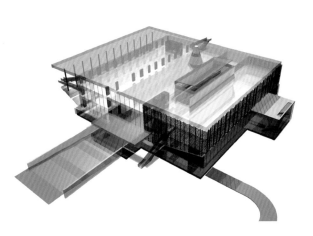

Paths

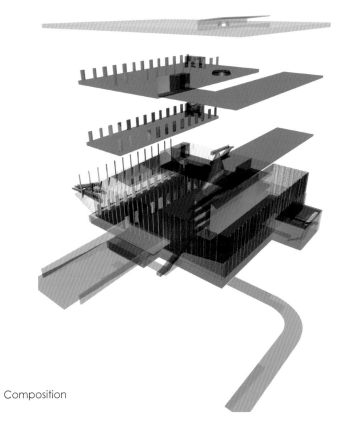

Composition

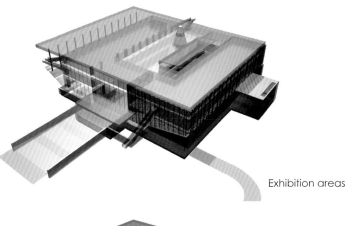

Exhibition areas

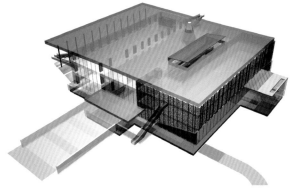

Coverage

1870 War Museum of Gravelotte

View of the building

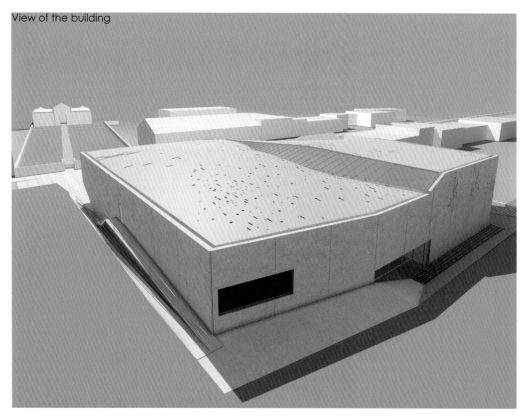

Location: Gravelotte, France **Designer:** Serero Architects
Photographer: Serero Architects **Competition Date:** 2009
Competition Name: Competition for 1870 War Museum
of Gravelotte **Construction Area:** 3,500 sqm **Place in the
Competition:** 1st Prize

Awarded reason:
The new 1870 War Museum of Gravelotte is
a building of high energy and environmental
performance.

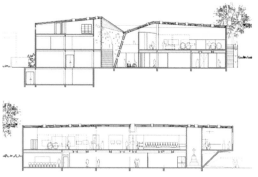

The proposition for the new War Museum of
Gravelotte stages the violence of the fights, by
appropriating the traces of the war to transform
them into an architectural effect. In the lobby
volume, which structures the whole museum, the
designers conceived an architectural device,
consisting of random perforations of the walls
and roof of the museum to let penetrate natural
light and on the other hand a "collapse" of the
roof into the hall. The natural light plays here
a fundamental role in the perception of the
museum spaces. It is channelled by a system of
hundreds perforation of different sizes and forms.
Such as light "cannon", they bombard the space
of the hall with a rain of sunrays, the intensity and
direction of which vary according to the hour of
the day.
The museum opens up at the level of the
reception hall by a large glass curtain wall onto
the public plaza. The geometry of the building,
a square with two cut sides, allows to align the
façades of the museum with two views of the site:
the view on the historical hall of memory and the
view on the Gravelotte's battlefields.

Urban insertion

View from exterior court

Display area

Hall of the museum

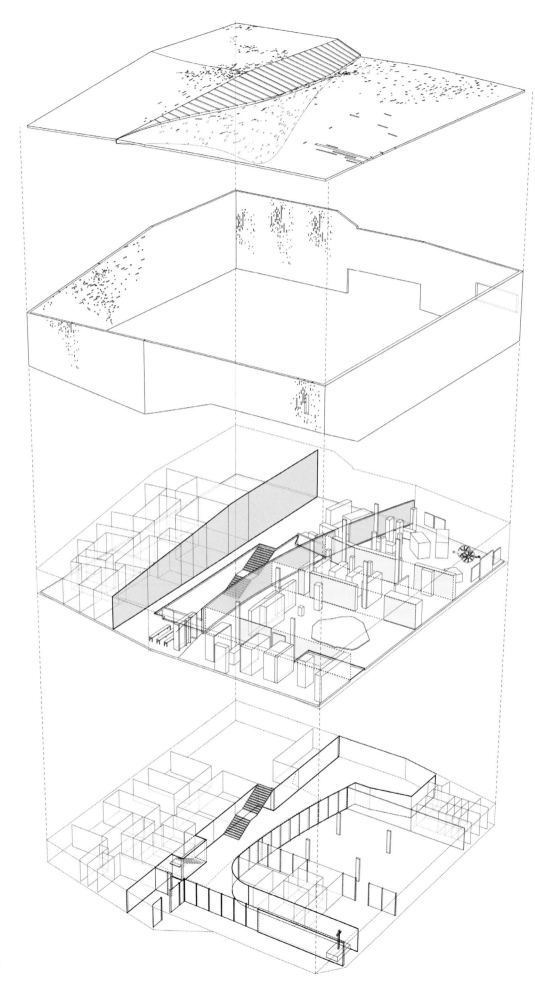

Axonometric drawing

218

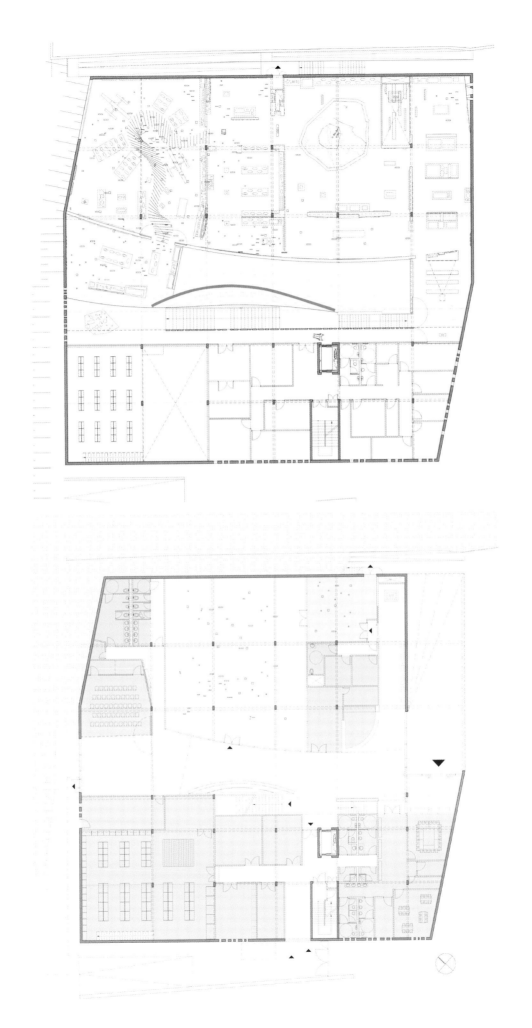

Macedonian Fight Museum

Location: Stockholm, Sweden **Designer:** Kjellgren Kaminsky Architecture **Photographer:** Kjellgren Kaminsky Architecture **Competition Date:** 2008 **Competition Name:** International Competition for Macedonian Fight Museum **Construction Area:** 5,100 sqm **Place in the Competition:** 1st Prize

Awarded reason:
The new museum both adapts to its surroundings and interprets them in new ways.

The building is made up of only a few strong elements: the transparent façade, the ramps and the central wall. The façade is made up of thin sheets of marble filtering the natural light. On certain carefully chosen spots the façade is punctuated by transparent glass offering views of important historical places in the surroundings. The building is constructed with concrete slabs held up by pillars along the façades. The slabs span 12 metres from the central wall to the façades. The heavy central wall together with the slabs and pillars gives the building seismic stability. The stone slab façade is constructed as a curtain wall façade.

In the exhibition hall, the central wall constitutes the bulk of the exhibition and here one may follow the chronology of events illustrated by pictures and movies projected on the wall. Along the façade smaller rooms contain more specialised exhibitions concerning certain events, with a view of historical areas of Skopje as a backdrop. Left is a generous flexible area, which can be arranged in different ways depending on the type of material being exhibited. Between the two exhibitions is a common room that can host joint activities and functions as electronic information centre.

The transparent façade

View from the river

Sections

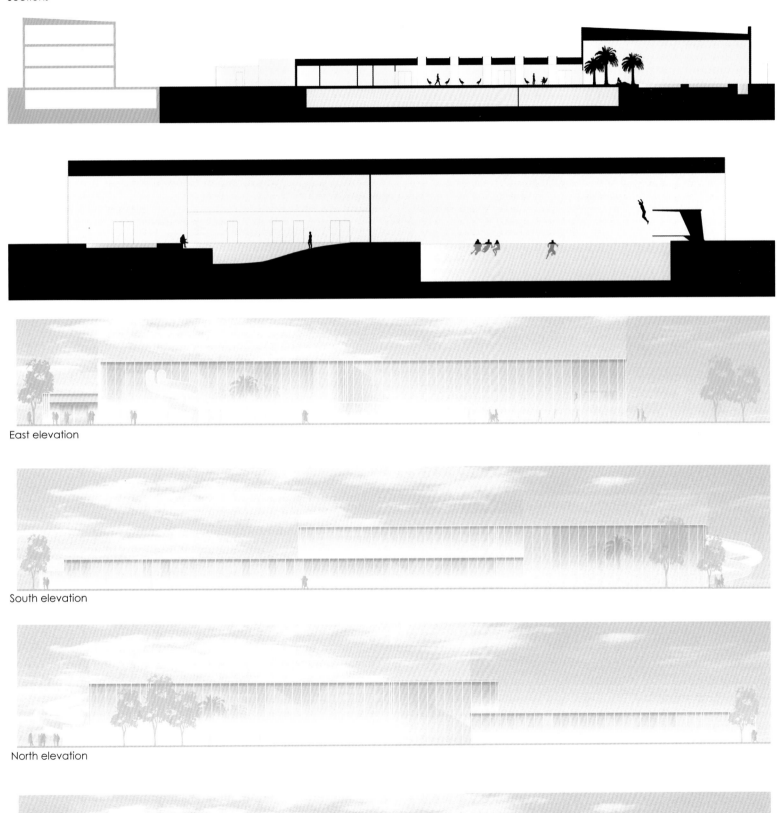

East elevation

South elevation

North elevation

West elevation

Museum of Tolerance in Jerusalem

Location: Jerusalem, Israel **Designer:** Chyutin Architects
Competition Date: 2010 **Competition Name:** The New
Museum of Tolerance in Jerusalem Competition **Site
Area:** 6,000 sqm **Construction Area:** 15,000 sqm **Place in
the Competition:** 1st Prize

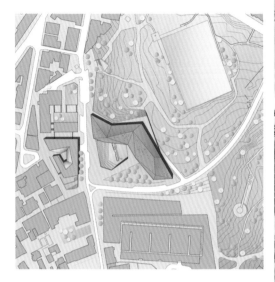

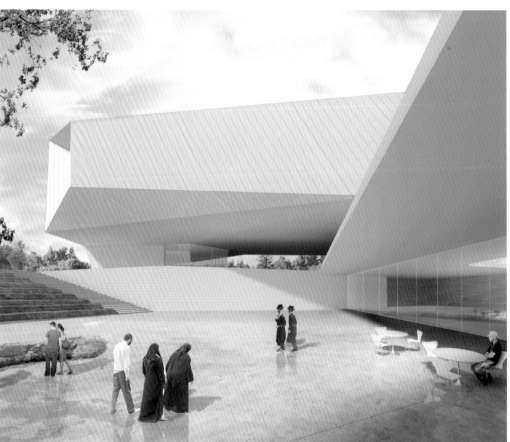

The Museum of Tolerance is located at the
heart of modern Jerusalem, in its rejuvenated
city centre, on the borderline between the
spacious Independence Park, and the urban
built environment. The designers created an
elongated structure which traces the southern
and eastern borderline of the site. The structure
orchestrates the three surrounding streets, into a
coherent urban space – a new public square for
the rejuvenated city centre of Jerusalem.

The building is divided into two horizontal wings:
a three-floor floating upper wing which hosts the
theatre and social meeting spaces, and a two
floors lower sunken wing which hosts the children
and the adult museums exhibition spaces – the
so-called "dark box". The entrance floor located
at the level of the public square hosts a restaurant
and gift shop. The entrance floor is leading up
to the floating wing or down to the sunken one.
A four-level lobby connects the floating wing
and the sunken one. Part of the floating wing
is suspended over ground level, creating a
gap, a doorway, from the built city to the park.
Pedestrians who are relaxing in the public square
or walking towards the park may be enticed to
enter the MOTJ building and experience it.

Entrance

Upper lobby

Section

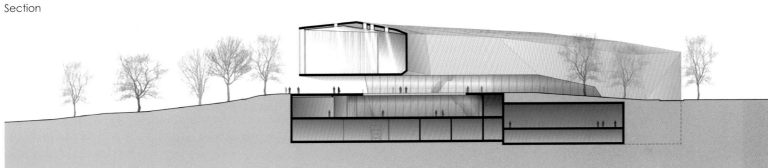

Section

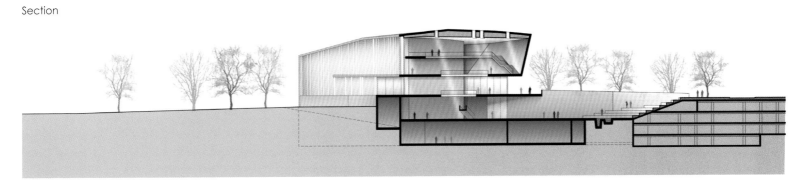

Section

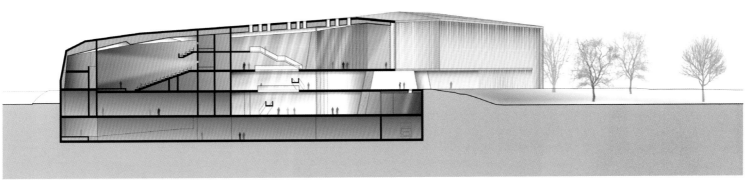

Entrance lobby

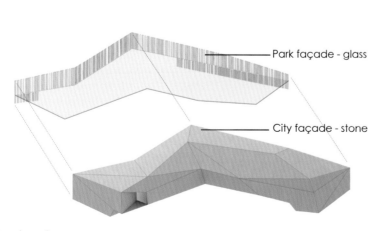

Archeological garden

Adult museum- "People's Journey"

Exhibits lift

Children's museum

Museum support

Staff entrance

Lecture rooms

Lower lobby & orientation

Docent's lounge

Vehicle entrance

Archeological garden level

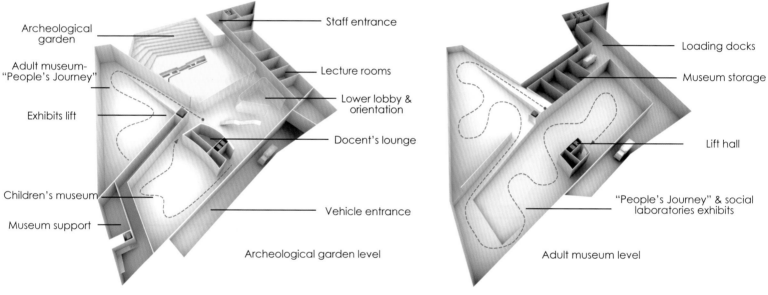

Loading docks

Museum storage

Lift hall

"People's Journey" & social laboratories exhibits

Adult museum level

Park façade - glass

City façade - stone

Façades scheme

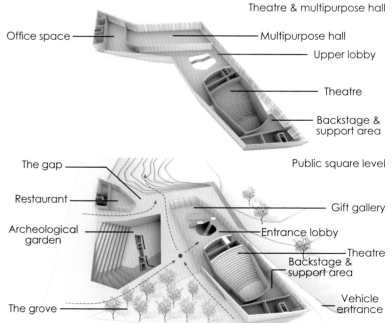

Theatre & multipurpose hall

Office space

Multipurpose hall

Upper lobby

Theatre

Backstage & support area

Public square level

The gap

Restaurant

Archeological garden

The grove

Gift gallery

Entrance lobby

Theatre

Backstage & support area

Vehicle entrance

228

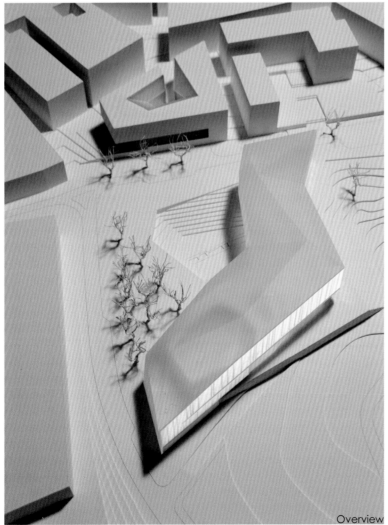

Overview

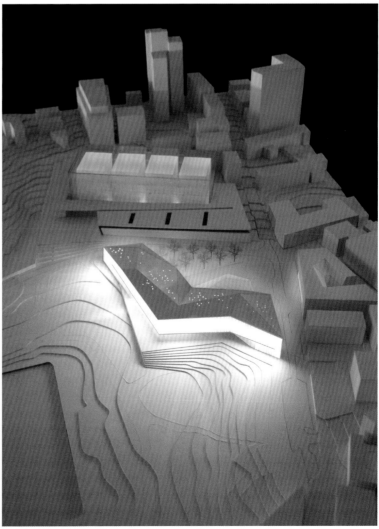

Pier Museum

Location: Miami, USA **Designer:** Arman Bahram, Donnie Duncanson, Abreowong Etteh, Brian Tobin, James White **Photographer:** Arman Bahram, Donnie Duncanson, BArch (hons) **Competition Date:** 2009 **Competition Name:** MIAMI 2009 Urban Competition – Pier Museum **Construction Area:** 2,000 sqm **Place in the Competition:** 3rd Prize

The proposal takes on the idea of Heterotopia (non-place) as a heuristic device in defining the museum as a pier that traverses the boundary conditions of the terrain and culminating at sea with a viewing platform. The spaces of the museum hinge off the axis of the main corridor as a series of points of exchange. As a means of telling the unfolding narratives of the emigrés and successive generations, the cultural commons hosts a broad range of events and activities to work in conjunction with the periodical exhibitions in the museum.

If the traditional museum operates on principles of preservation and permanence, then the Pier Museum celebrates the transient nature of the borrowed artefacts and the history they embody. As opposed to the traditional museum, all artefacts are only temporarily stored before they are assembled as formal displays.

Viewing platform

Bath/dance floor

Reception area

Longitudinal section

Level 2   Street

Level 1   Beach

Level 0   Underwater

Site plan

1   2   3   4   5   6   7   8   9

7   8   9

1   2 3   4   6
                   5   10

Sections

235

Nan Yue Museum

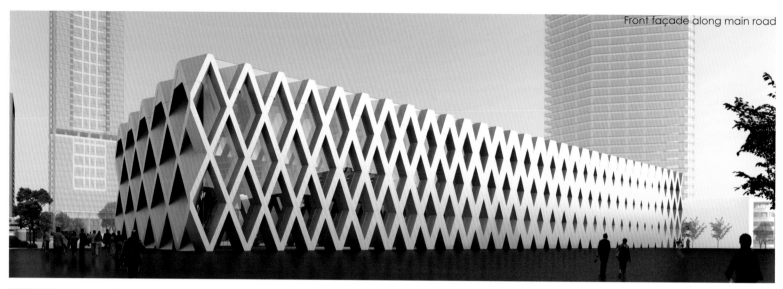

Front façade along main road

Entrance façade

Location: Guangzhou, China **Designer:** Information Based Architecture **Photographer:** Information Based Architecture **Competition Date:** 2008 **Competition Name:** International Competition for the Design of the Nan Yue Museum **Construction Area:** 10,000 sqm **Place in the Competition:** 1st Prize

Awarded reason:
The unique pattern and the inhabitable structure are excellent.

Through its abstract materiality and geometry the museum reflects the process of continuity of time and history. The façades of the museum, by showing a continuous densification, reflect how through the process of layering, a record of all that ever happened is stored in the earth. The lozenge pattern can be read as a pattern that is the result of being under compression of time. The resulting qualities that have been generated through historical layering and densification of the compression process happening over historical time are expressed in the museum as porosity, which is made productive as filtering and purifying.

The geometrical lozenge pattern that has been discovered on the tiles and stones coming from the 2,000-year-old Nan Yue period has been revived into a new modern lozenge pattern for the museum, creating a clear and recognisable face for the museum. The lozenge will be a crisp and bright logo that will reflect the importance of the region, and through its simplicity and clarity remind people of the 2,000-year-old history of the city of Guangzhou and underscore the important role that the city has played over time.

Aerial view

View over park

Museum façade on park side

Interior view of museum main hall over archeological findings

Interior view of upper museum spaces

240

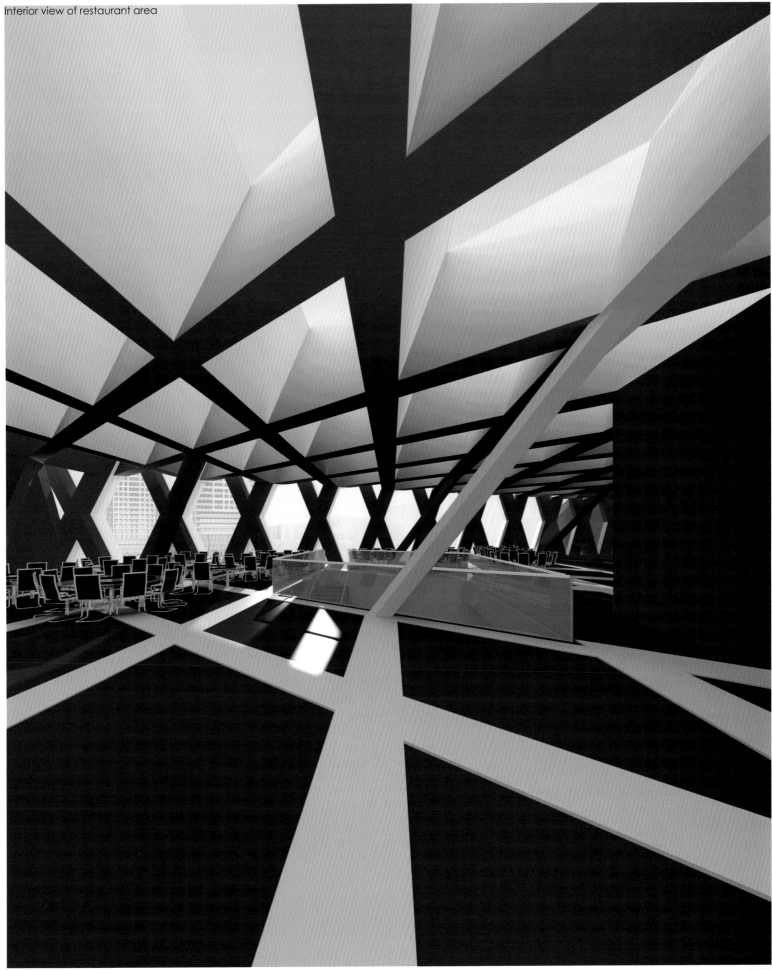

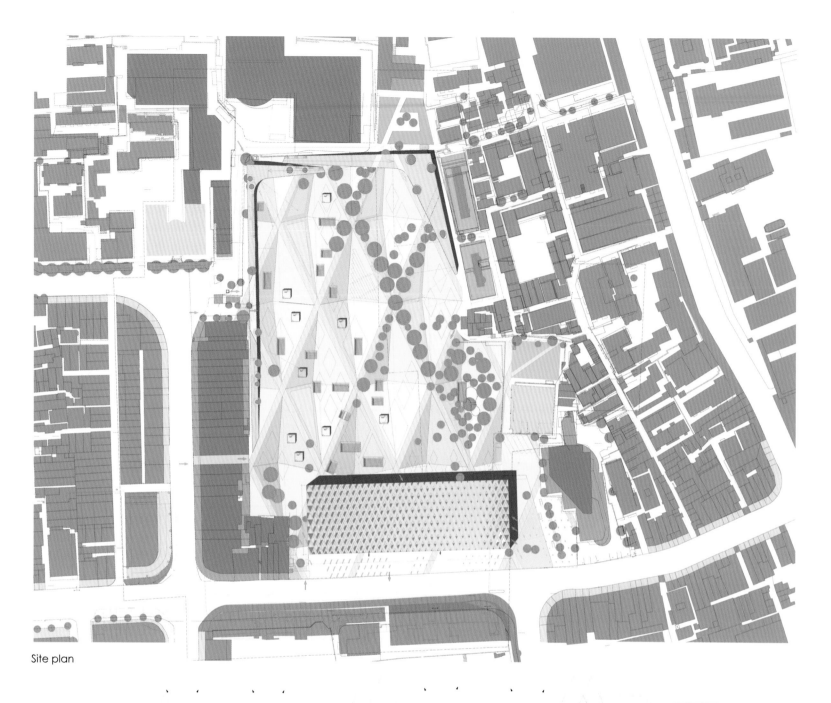

Site plan

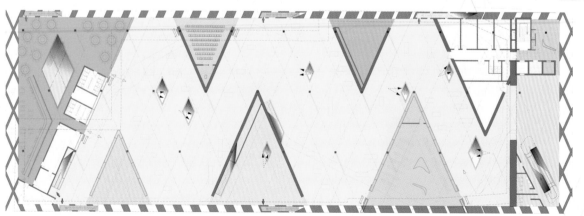

First floor plan

242

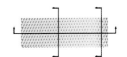

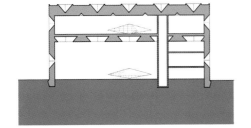

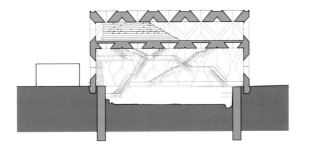

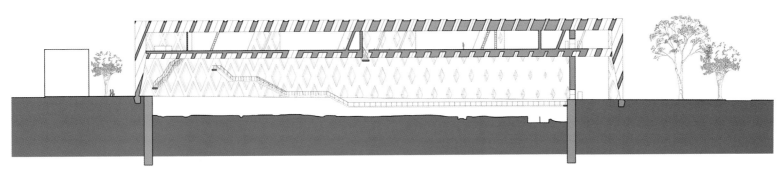

Sections

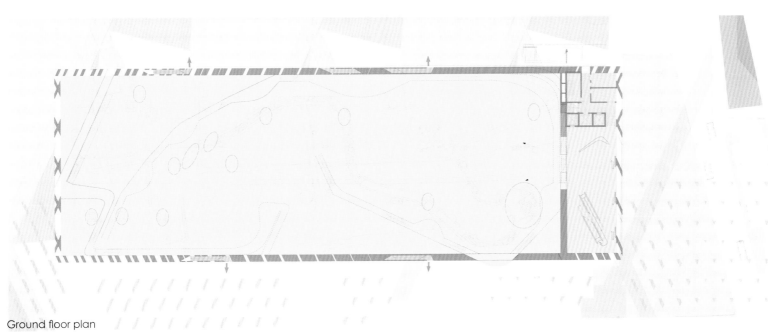

Ground floor plan

M9 Museum in Mestre

Location: Mestre, Italy **Designer:** Sauerbruch Hutton **Competition Date:** 2010 **Site Area:** 3,400 sqm **Construction Area:** 13,800 sqm **Place in the Competition:** 1st Prize

Together with the ex-stable, on the western side of the plot, for which is envisaged a project of restructuring for commercial purposes, the complex will also revitalise the part crossed by Calle Legrenzi. The existing path at ground level will be widened following an open corner towards the "Museum Square" in order to indicate the entrance even from a distance. The visitor's attention will be captured as they draw nearer on foot to the museum by the diagonal volumes of the two new bodies of the construction, whose entrances and whose internal organisation will be immediately discernible. The building is identifiable owing to its exterior cladding in polychrome ceramic.

View from the plaza

Main entrance

Exhibition hall

246

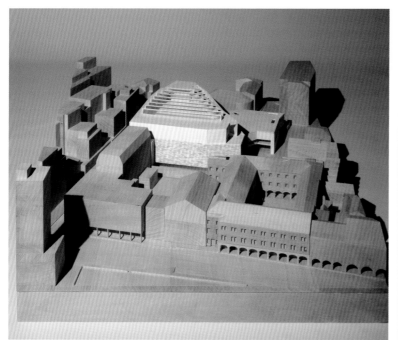

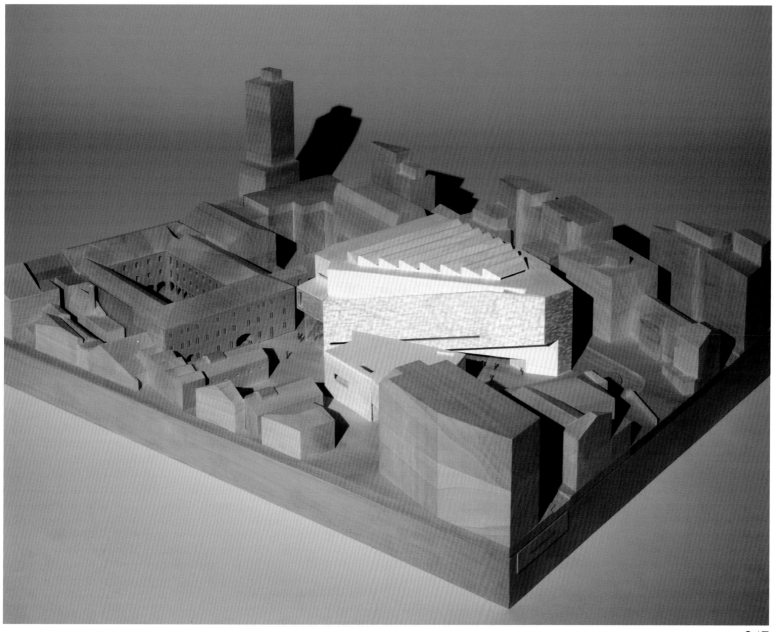

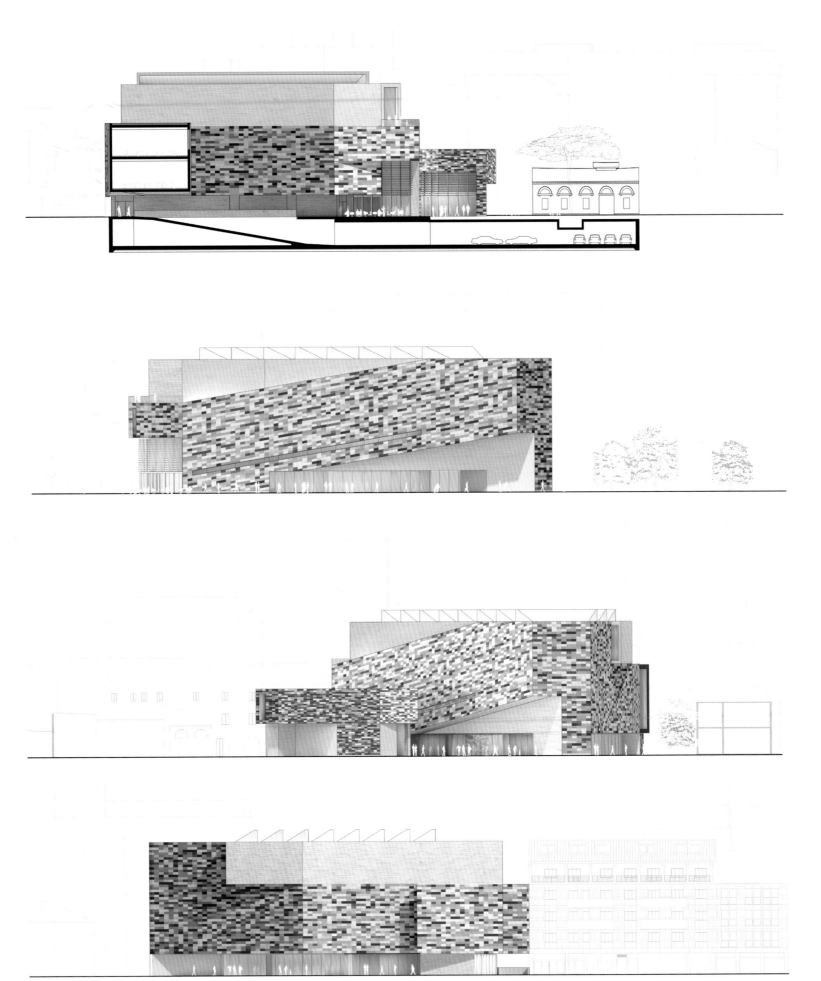

Elevations
248

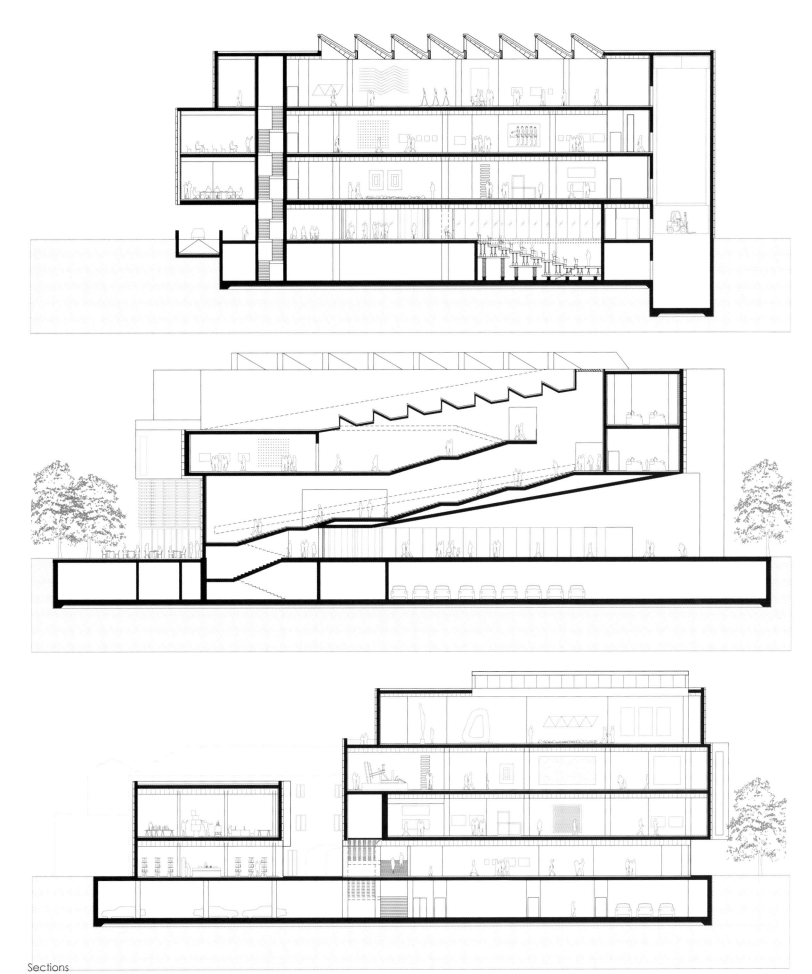

Sections

249

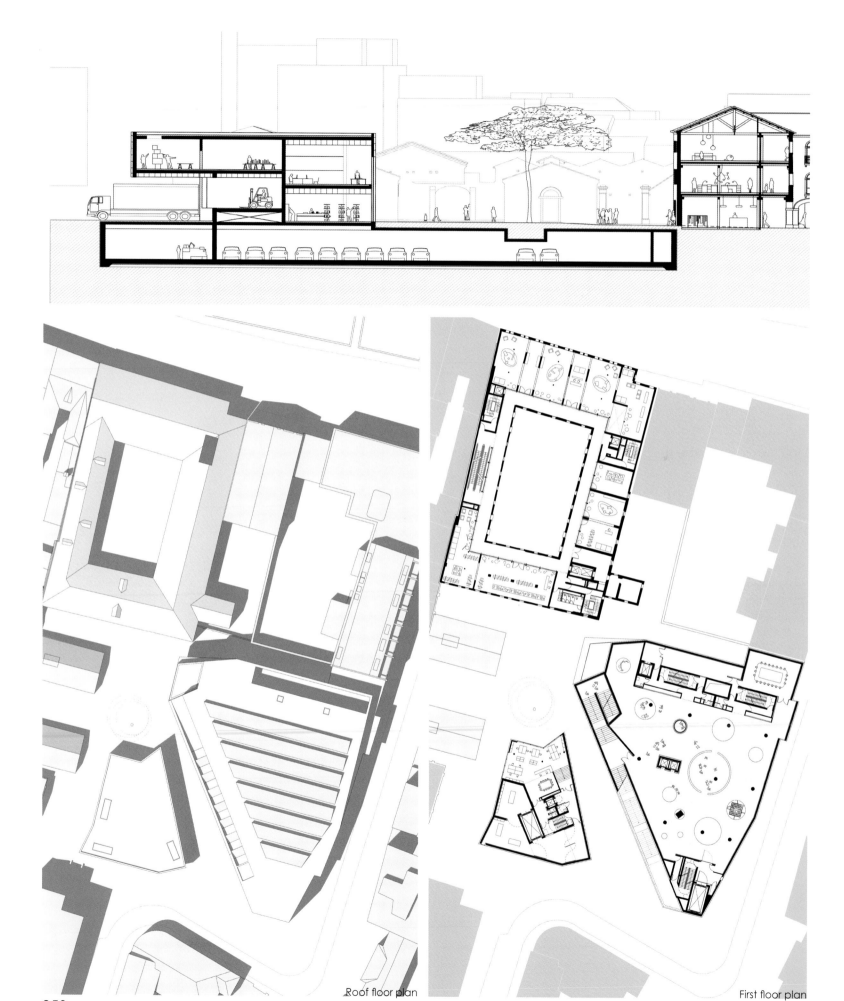

Roof floor plan

First floor plan

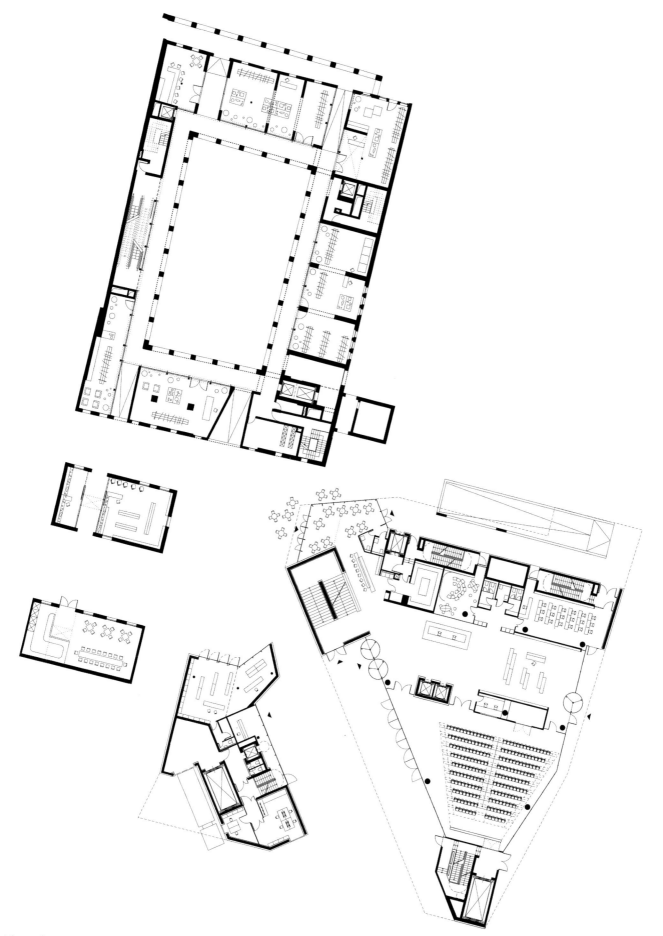

Ground floor plan

Tianjin Museum

Entry

Location: Tianjin, China **Designer:** Perkins+Will
Competition Date: 2009 **Competition Name:** International
Design Competition for the Tianjin Museum of Industry
and City History

This museum was designed as part of a design
competition for the master plan of a new museum
campus for the city of Tianjin. The concept of the
museum is based on an abstraction of a series of
historical elements which are key to the founding
of Tianjin. The water and pedestrian walkways
that surround the museum recall the saltern beds
which were part of the salt industry that was and
still is one of the major industries of Tianjin. The
crystalline form of salt is also the inspiration for the
façade system and atrium. The "Crystal Atrium"
forms the grand preface hall and rises above the lower
scale massing of the main building as a focal point. The
façade system, which consists of individually cast
translucent glass cubes, will react with natural
lighting conditions to enliven the presence of the
museum within its context.

View from southeast

252

View from north

View from northeast

254

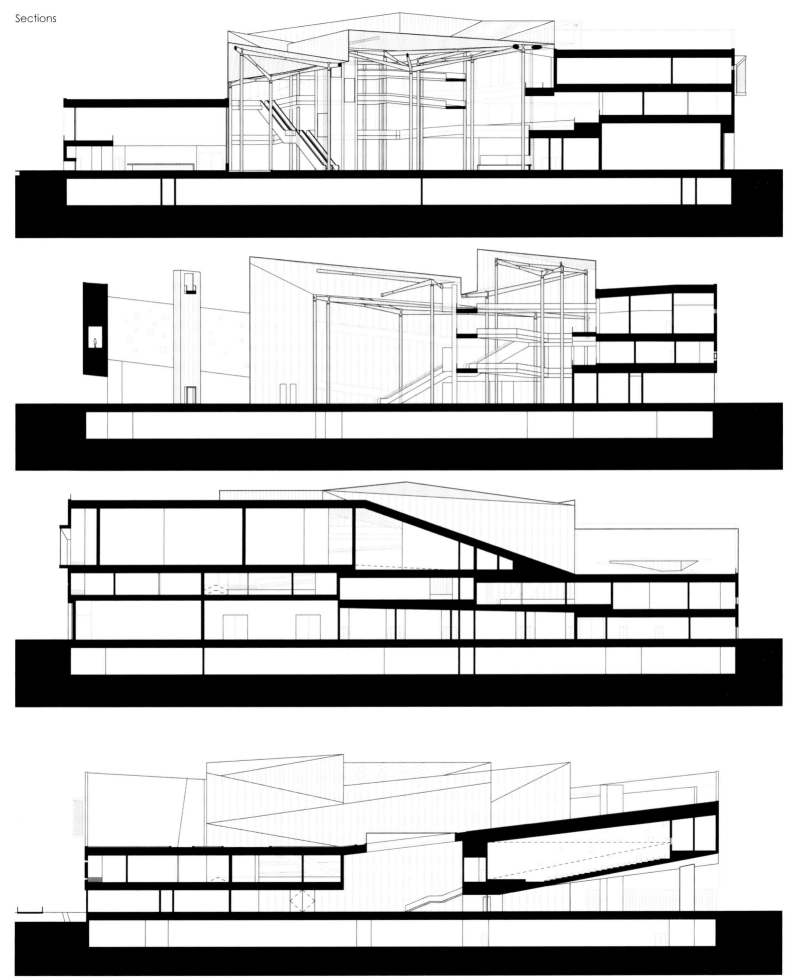

Ground floor plan

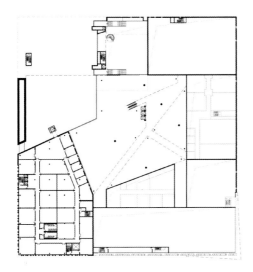

First floor plan

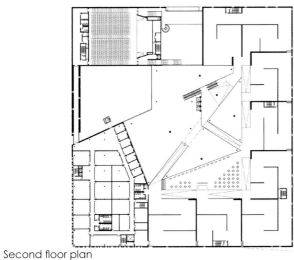

Second floor plan

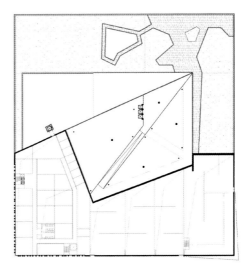

Third floor plan

Fourth floor plan

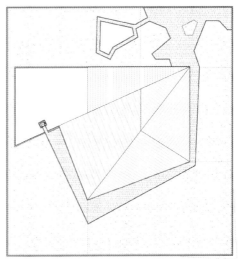

Roof floor plan

257

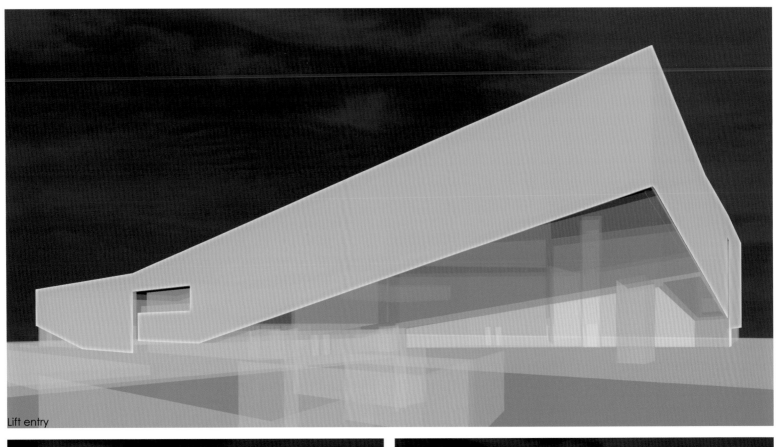
Lift entry

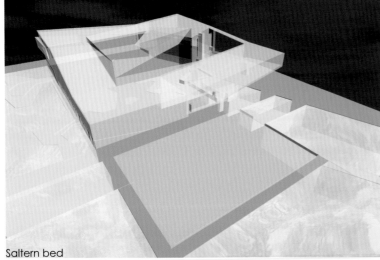
Saltern bed

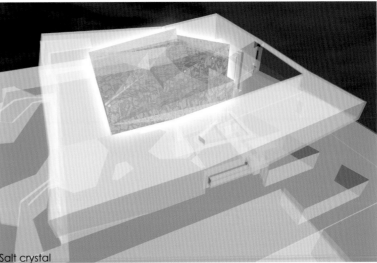
Salt crystal

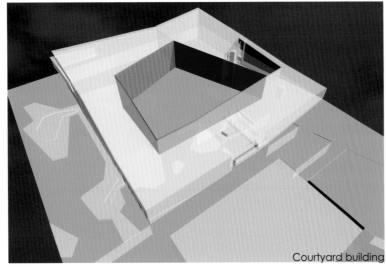
Courtyard building

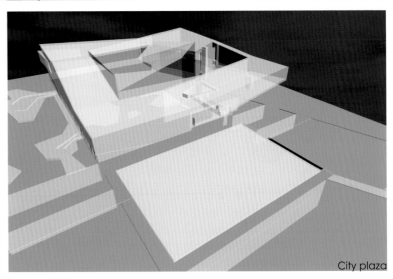
City plaza

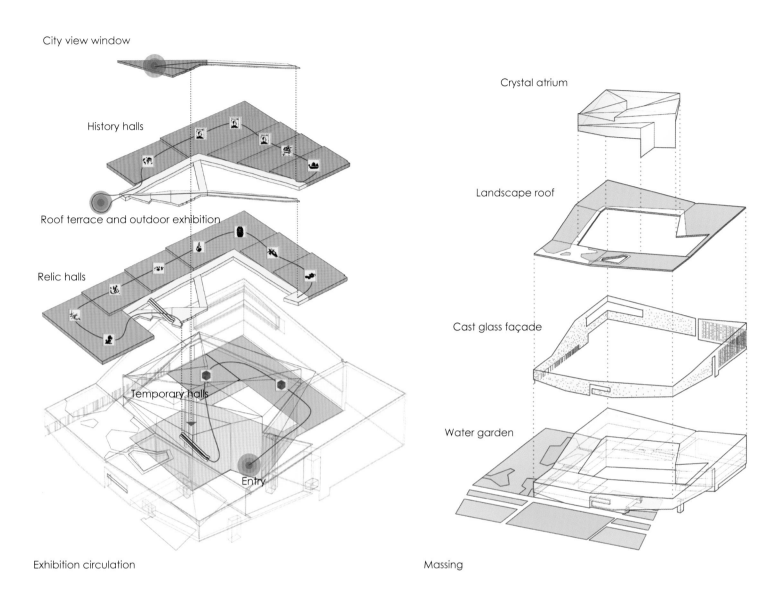

City view window

History halls

Roof terrace and outdoor exhibition

Relic halls

Temporary halls

Entry

Exhibition circulation

Crystal atrium

Landscape roof

Cast glass façade

Water garden

Massing

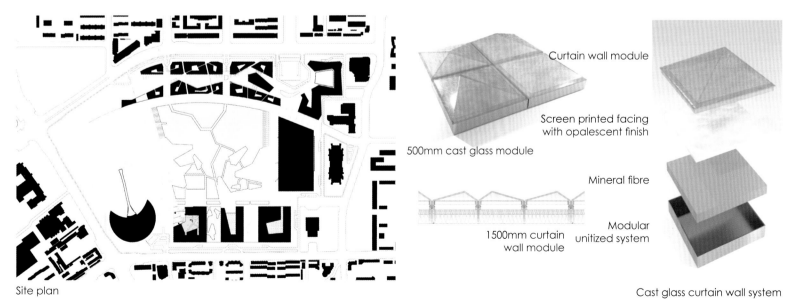

Site plan

Curtain wall module

Screen printed facing
with opalescent finish

500mm cast glass module

Mineral fibre

Modular
unitized system

1500mm curtain
wall module

Cast glass curtain wall system

Tianjin Museum of Industry and City History

Aerial view

Location: Tianjin, China **Designer:** ABSTRAKT Studio Architecture/Voytek Gorczynski Architect **Photographer:** ABSTRAKT Studio Inc./Voytek Gorczynski Architect **Competition Date:** 2004 **Competition Name:** International Design Competition for the Tianjin Museum of Industry and City History **Construction Area:** 32,000 sqm **Place in the Competition:** 2nd Prize

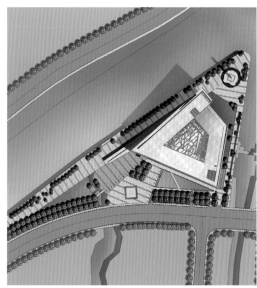

Water's edge walkway

The architectural concept of the Museum has been informed by two key factors: the prominent location of the site and the symbolic character of the building within the city of Tianjin. The site is located on the junction of the Ziya River and South Canal, which forms a prow with the historic Monument commemorating construction of the new canal on its end. Surrounded by water on two sides, the site calls for a building, which organically grows from it and is symbolically related to it.

Both of the factors are addressed by massing the building in such a way that it becomes an intrinsic element of the site. Visitors will be able to experience the Museum not only by visiting its collection, but also will be able to walk along the building on the perimeter walkway located on the roof of the building. The walkway will be directly accessible from the water's edge boardwalk and will lead to the viewing platform located at the highest point of the Museum. The massing of the building expresses the notion of progress in history and positive development. Spiral geometry suggests that in Time and Space one can be at the same two-dimensional location but at the higher level in third and fourth dimension.

Main entrance

Main entrance plaza

View from South Canal

Exterior

Exterior

Exterior

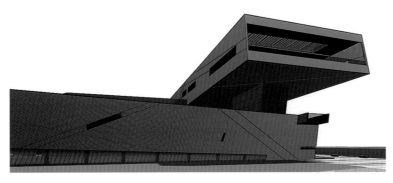

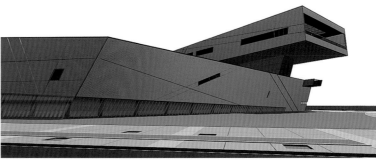

Exterior

Exterior

Exterior

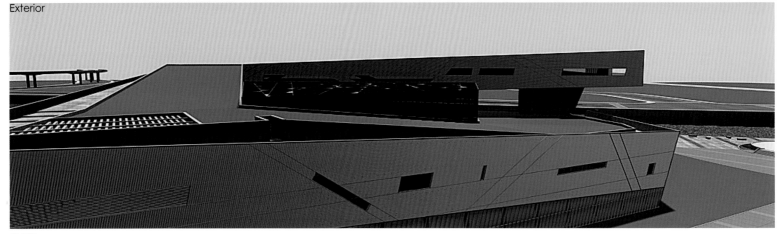

Temporary exhibition space

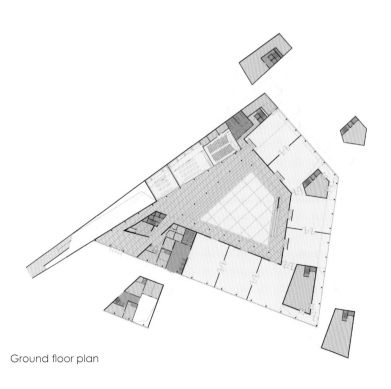

Ground floor plan

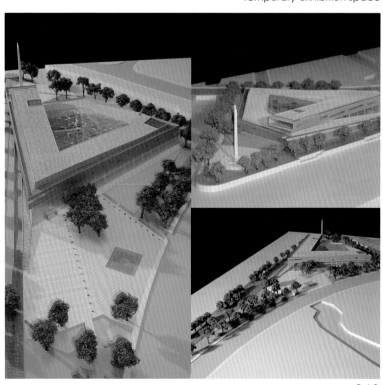

South elevation

West elevation

North elevation

East elevation

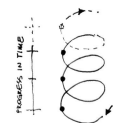

Spiral of progress

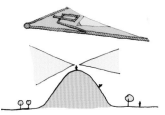

Building integrated with landscape

City views as part of museum experience

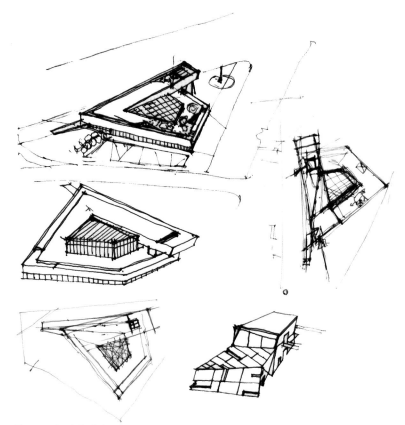

Conceptual sketches

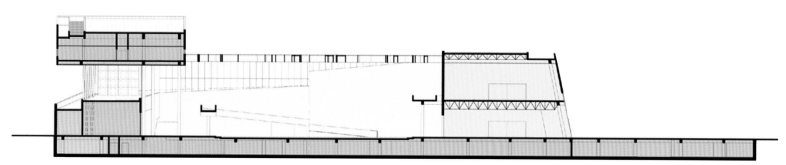

Section

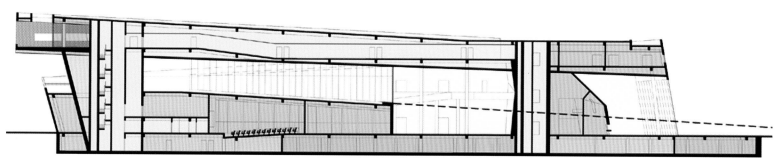

Section

Shandong Museum

Location: Jinan, China **Designer:** Jourdan & Müller (Benjamin Jourdan), Beijing Institute of Architectural Design **Competition Date:** 2007 **Competition Name:** New Shandong Museum Proposal International Competition **Place in the Competition:** 1st Prize

Awarded reason:
A proposal with great innovative character

The architectural form shows a distinctive context to the Chinese culture and is developed from Chinese writing and calligraphy. Chinese writing is consequently one of the cultural connector to the 21ˢᵗ century. It is connecting symbolicalness and content as a phrase of multifaceted and creative Chinese culture. Confucius, one of the most famous sons of the province of Shandong, was a mentor concerning world order and life-form. A lot of writers and academics followed him and developed Chinese calligraphy as a kind of philosophy of life. The gesture of writing hands, the movement of life deposited as a dynamic building-form in the 21ˢᵗ century. The museum personified this issue. A lot of folding affected the sculptural form of the building. The urbanistic arrangement including the museum of science is like a abstraction of a stroke of a brush. A place of culture is connecting the city and mountains with sanctify places in the north and south which are embossed by the Yellow River. The place becomes a "window into nature" which is surrounding the museum.

Overview

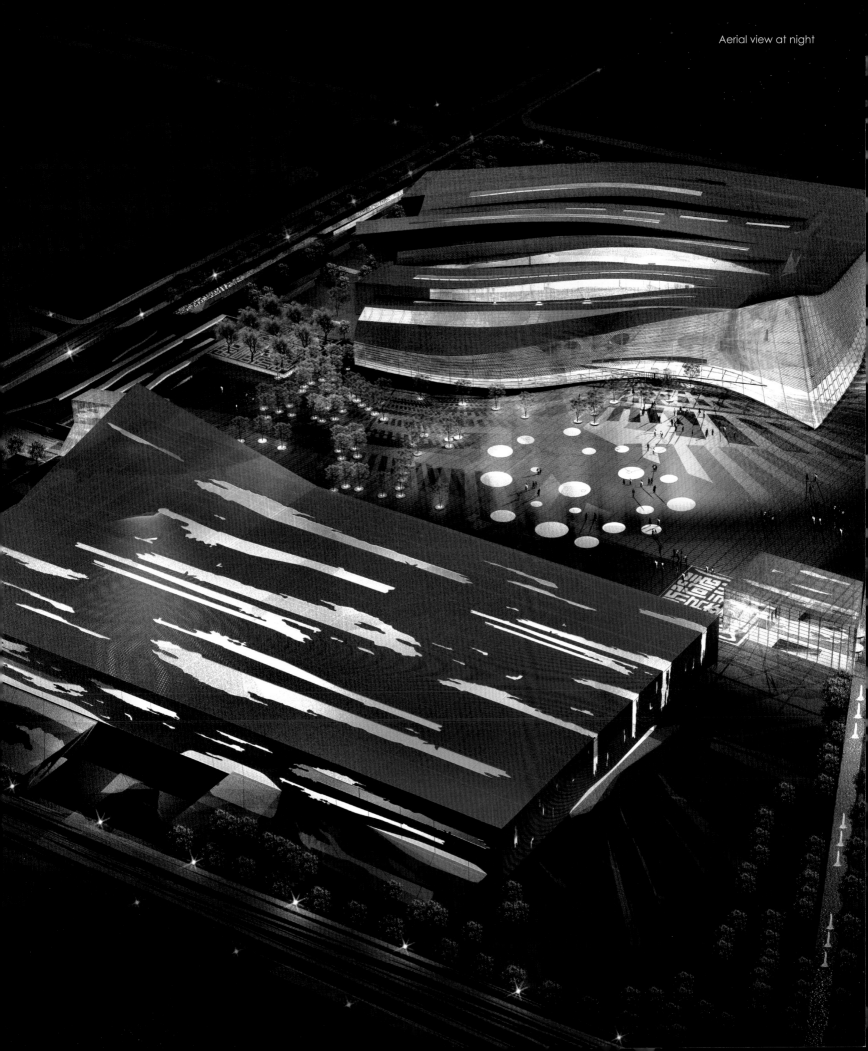

Specimen of marine life display area

Vessels and model ships display area

Dinosaur fossil display area

Buddhist sculpture display area

Lounge

268

Square perspective

Site plan

Ground floor plan

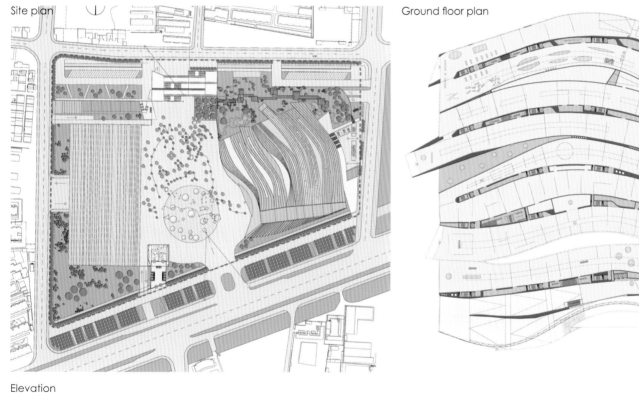

Elevation

Elevation

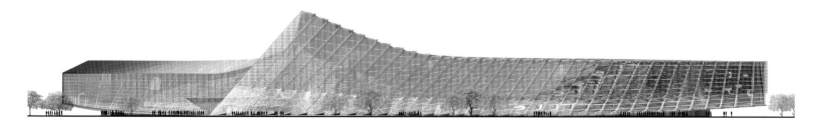

Index

5+1AA
Interiano 3/11-16124 Genova
Tel: +39 010 540095
Fax: +39 010 5402094

3Gatti Architecture Studio
via de' Ciancaleoni 34, 00184
Rome, Italy
Tel: +39 06 45 22 13 589
Fax: +39 17 82 29 93 21

**ABSTRAKT Studio Architecture/
Voytek Gorczynski Architect**
180 Belsize Dr. M4S 1M1 Toronto
Canada
Tel: +416 830 3160
Fax: +416 484 6495

**Bélanger Beauchemin Morency
architects**
819, avenue Moreau Québec
(Québec), G1V 3B5, Canada
Tel: +418 653 8341
Fax: +418 653 1989

BIG
Nørrebrogade 66D, 2nd Floor
2200 Copenhagen N
Denmark
Tel: +45 7221 7227

Chyutin Architects
12 Taiber Street, 53415 Givataim
Israel
Tel: +972 0 3 7320064
Fax: +972 0 3 7312760

Corsi Hirano Arquitetos
Rua General Jardim, 645-S92 Villa
Buarque 01223-011, Sao Paulo,
Brazil
Tel: +55 11 3120 5986

Dorell.Ghotmeh.Tane/Architects
6 rue Desargues, 75011 Paris
France
Tel: +33 1 43 38 12 47
Fax: +33 1 43 38 12 85

ELEMENTAL
Los Conquistadores 1700 Piso
25-A Providencia, Santiago, Chile
Tel: +56 2 753 3000
Fax: +56 2 753 3016

Gerasimos Pavlidis
Tel: +30 2310 831256
Fax: +30 693 7036803

Guinée*Potin Architects
13 allée de l'île Gloriette
44 000 Nantes, France
Tel: +02 40 73 38 13
Fax: +02 44 84 59 40

HerrerosArquitectos
Calle Princesa 25, El
Hexágono, 28008 Madrid, Spain
Tel: +34 915 22 77 69
Fax: +34 915 59 46 78

Information Based Architecture
Stavangerweg 890, Studio 29,
1013 AX, Amsterdam
The Netherlands
Tel: +31 20 6366222
Fax: +31 20 6366222

Jourdan & Müller
Gräfstrasse 79, 60486 Frankfurt am
Main, Germany
Tel: +49 69 970818 0
Fax: +49 69 970818 11

Kimmel Eshkolot Architects
27 Chelouche St., Tel Aviv 65149
Israel
Tel: +972 3 5176059
Fax: +972 3 5100950

Kjellgren Kaminsky Architecture
Ekmansgatan 3, 411 32
Göteborg, Sweden
Tel: +46 0 31 761 20 01
Fax: +46 0 31 18 21 04

KSP JÜRGEN ENGEL ARCHITEKTEN
Hanauer Landstraße 287-289
60314 Frankfurt am Main
Germany
Tel: +49 0 69 94 43 94 0
Fax: +49 0 69 94 43 94 0

LABSCAPE Architecture
392 Broadway (2nd Floor)
New York, NY10013, USA
Tel: +1 646 707 3871
Fax: +1 646 596 9368

LAN Architecture
25 Rue d'Hauteville, 75010 Paris
France
Tel: +33 1 43 70 00 60
Fax: +33 1 43 70 01 21

Logon Ltd.
Marburger Strasse 2, 10789 Berlin
Germany
Tel: +49 30 85 99 46 188
Fax: +49 30 85 99 46 100

LOOS ARCHITECTS & bureau SLA
Wilgenweg 20-B, 1031 HV
Amsterdam, The Netherlands
Tel: +31 0 20 3300128
Fax: +31 0 20 6207600

Manuelle Gautrand
36, Boulevard de la Bastille
75003 Paris, France
Tel: +33 0 156 950 646

OFIS Architect
Tavcarjeva 2,1000 Ljubljana
Slovenia
Tel: +386 1 4260084
Fax: +386 1 4260085

Perkins+Will
330 North Wabash Avenue, Suite
3600, Chicago, IL 60611, USA
Tel: +1 312 755 0770
Fax: +1 312 755 0775

Preston Scott Cohen, Inc.
179 Sidney Street, 1st Floor
Cambridge, MA02139, USA
Tel: +617 441 2110
Fax: +617 441 2113

REX
20 Jay Street Suite 920, Brooklyn
NY 11201, USA
Tel: +1 646 230 6557

RICE+LIPKA ARCHITECTS
40 Worth Street, Suite 828, New
York, NY 10013, USA
Tel: +1 212 285 1003
Fax: +1 212 285 1005

Rodeo arkitekter
Youngstorget 2a, N-0181 Oslo
Norway
Tel: +47 99 64 03 64

Saucier + Perrotte architects
7043 Waverly, Montréal Québec,
Canada H2S 3J1
Tel: +514 273 1700
Fax: +514 273 3501

Sauerbruch Hutton
Lehrter Straße 57, D - 10557 Berlin
Germany
Tel: +49 30 397 821 0
Fax: +49 30 397 821 30

Serero Architects
136 Avenue Parmentier
75011 Paris, France
Tel: +33 01 45 08 14 31
Fax: +33 01 53 01 09 55

UNOAUNO – spazio architettura
Viaflaiano 1565015 Pescara
Italy
Tel: +085 2192063
Fax: +085 7992899

Yooshin Architects & Engineers
#453-2, Jindallae
bldg(2F, 3F, 4F), Dogok-dong,
Gangnam-gu, Seoul, Korea
Tel: +02 3462 5121
Fax: +02 3462 0452

Zerafa Architecture Studio
286 Spring Street, Suite 201
New York 10013, USA
Tel: +212 966 7083
Fax: +212 966 7086